Unbridling

The

American

Spirit

The Building Blocks of a Meaningful Life

Mark Fierle

Unbridling the American Spirit

Published by Solutions Press

© 2017 Mark Fierle
All rights reserved

First edition printed March 2017

ISBN: 978-0-9846872-5-1

Printed in the United States of America

This is a work of non-fiction. The ideas presented are those of the author alone. All references to possible results discussed in this book relate to specific past examples and are not neces-sarily representative of any future results specific individuals may achieve.

In his latest book my old college classmate Mark Fierle, takes a fresh look at what it takes to lead a meaningful life in our globalized society. A seasoned businessman, entrepreneur and author, Mark pulls no punches and tells it like it is. When I started reading, I couldn't put it down. Starting with I got a college degree but can't get a damn job, to when our dreams go south. Mark offers real life examples that show how others have gained or regained the path to a meaningful life. There is food for thought for every stage of your life, just starting out or even retired, *Unbridling the American Spirit* offers inspiration and resources that are meaningful for all. I highly recommend this book. Get out your highlighter and be prepared to be inspired.

Jim Weber, Founder and CEO
of Wyvern Technologies, Inc,
Silver Star recipient

Don't wait to talk to your child about what they want to do when they grow up. Begin in first grade and instill in them the confidence that they can achieve their dreams! This combined with Mark's reality will result in a successful individual you can be proud of; and, they themselves proud of whom they have become.

Cathy Fresch, Director of Development,
Gannon University

Thanks for the acknowledgement, Mark! I like how clear the writing is- it feels like I'm listening to you give an inspirational talk. I reflected back to college and my first internships/job/ mentors this would be a good book for students to read.

Irvin Huang, BS Engineering
MBA UC Irvine, Radio Talk Show Host

Unbridling the American Spirit embraces everything from choosing a Major (for parent or student) to becoming a valued team member and leader. Mark Fierle calls them as he sees them, challenging you to improve and lead all your life. Success stories, suggestions, ideas and the power of notes will fuel your self-improvement.

Steve Amos Engineer, Author

Mark Fierle has been a source of ideas and inspiration for me (and I'm sure for many others) for quite a few years. I've found that the questions he raises not only pique my interest, they tend to instigate some very spirited discussions. I find his points of view well-reasoned and insightful and usually expressed in ways that are easy to understand. This is a credit to his integrity and passion in confronting the truth. It is my hope that he continues to explore and report, as those efforts are not only beneficial to those of us who value his perspectives, but a tribute his wisdom and character.

Murray Schrantz, USMA, Engineer and Author

Unbridling the American Spirit is for educators, students, parents, entrepreneurs, consultants and anyone who wants to live rather than just exist. His human-interest stories lend credence to every point he shares. Whether the chapter on "Beards and Tattoos in the Workplace, when our dreams go south, or linear vs three-dimensional thinking, you will be able to find new ideas for living a more fulfilling life.

Kay Vickory, Consultant

Contents

Foreword v

Dedication vii

Part I Meaningful Education 1

I've Got a College Degree, But I Can't Get a Damn Job! 1

College Grads Can't Get the Right Job 1

Students Don't Select Majors Wisely.................................. 1

Reality is Brutal 2

What About the College Elders?.................................... 3

College Administrators Are Also Out of Touch........................ 4

Example of a Person Who Chose Wisely.............................. 7

Beards and Tattoos in The Workplace 9

Choosing Majors 10

Guidelines for Parents with Students About to Enter the World

of Higher Education 11

Part II Continuous Self-Improvement 15

Food for Thought- Who Has the Remote Control? 17

Comparing Yourself with Others 18

Intimidation and Fear.. 22

Speaking in Public 24

Part III Success Story Updates 27

The Story of Officer Robert Pedregon 29

The Day I Almost Quit Being a Police Officer 32

Another Update: The Doc and The Girl............................. 35

Part IV Leadership and Mentorship.......................... 39

Transforming Your Life... 41

Continuing Education Thoughts 43

A Few More Things to Consider....................................... 44

How Do We Decide? 46

History of The Car Radio.. 47

What's in a Name?.. 49

Making Life Matter - A Cake of Yeast................................ 51

Are You a Prima Donna or Essential Incompetent? 53

Essential Incompetents 54

Tips to Improve and Become a Competent 56

Prima Donnas 58

The Value of Saying No 61

The Value of Learning to be a Leader 62

Leadership and Mentor Training 63

What Should We Do If We Are a New Manager? 63

What is a Mentor? 64

Leadership: Teams and Teammates 70

The Fallacy of Being Perfect 72

When Our Dreams Go South 77

What Can We Do? 78

Attitude Counts 80

Other Benefits 80

Keeping at It 83

Code of Conduct 85

Linear Vs Three-Dimensional Thinking 92

Some People Exist, Some People Live 94

Get to Know Mark Fierle 97

Foreword

The mustang in all its forms has always been an iconic symbol of freedom and the American spirit.

The Mustang horse I included on the front cover is a timeless symbol of the cowboy of the old west.

The P51 Mustang airplane enabled the American Air Force to dominate the theatre of war in Europe and Asia during WW2. My father-in-law tells a story about the P51 saving his ass more than once while flying a B24 bomber in the Pacific during WW2. Again, it is an iconic symbol of the American way.

Then comes the Mustang car the Ford Motor company developed in 1964, which changed the auto industry in America and to this day brings a smile to anyone talking about cars.

The back outside cover of this book includes a picture of both a P51 and my personal Mustang car. A friend recently asked me, "How many miles per gallon do you get?" I nonchalantly replied, "Six Camaros per gallon!" Whoa!

This book is divided into four parts. I call them the *Building Blocks of a Meaningful Life*, as I see them. I don't claim they are the only four, they are the ones I want to touch on here.

1) Meaningful education. Anyone can say, "I studied this or that and have a Bachelor's, Master's or Doctorate." Don't get me wrong. You can study whatever you want. It is only important if you get meaningful value from it. Meaningful education opens a new world that will help you achieve an objective. Otherwise it is just information, useful or not!

2) Continuous self-improvement. If you do not work to improve all your life, you can become less meaningful, even a has-been. We have a long life to be useful to society, family, and friends.

Improvement means taking on new projects, finding new ways to help not only yourself but others. Countless people have done this long after they retired from regular jobs. They volunteered, learned how to write or speak, created countless projects that give meaning to their life far beyond advancing up the corporate ladder or making more money.

3) Updates on stories of success after major setbacks. I first shared many of these stories in my book, *Rekindling the American Dream.* Now, three years later, we find out what happened since and how each fared. These compelling stories give examples of how you can overcome odds and achieve your dreams by unbridling your American spirit. What's your story?

4) Leadership and mentoring is the fourth building block. While much has been written on leadership, several interesting aspects are unique. I have never seen much dialogue as is heard around the water cooler or at cocktail hour.

Dedication

I dedicate this book to my immediate family, who put up with my ruminations and frustrations as I completed this project. They have been very helpful and patient with me.

I also dedicate this book to my colleagues in our Business and Communication group. They include Lee Pound, my editor and writing teacher; John Hall; Steve Amos, who always keeps me on track; Christine Wong, a Master Gardener friend living in Hawaii; Kay Vickery, who always gets it right; Vince Glaeser with his input on higher education; and Murray Schrantz.

Also, thank you to Irvin Huang, fellow talk show host at KUCI 88.9 FM in Irvine and a recent engineering grad and Masters student, for his input from the millennial viewpoint.

Thanks to all. Without your input and help on the rewrite this would not be possible.

Three years ago, I started this project. Yes, three freakin' years. Along the way ideas have bugged me. After writing down my ideas, I filled in the blanks. First, I did onerous research then interviewed dozens of people. At times, I shut it all down and let the book bake in the oven. My constant thought became: Is this meaningful?

I decided yes and continued my work. While you may not agree with all my ideas, I ask you to open your mind and consider them. That is what makes great discussions.

If you buy the softcover edition, keep your hi-lighter and pencil nearby. Don't be afraid to mark up the book with your comments. They will create fruitful discussions in the future.

I am interested in what you think. You can reach me at mfassoci@aol.com. You can purchase my books on Amazon.com in either softcover or e-book format. Be sure to read *Rekindling the American Dream* and *Adapt or Perish,* available in both softcover and e-book formats on amazon.com.

Part I

Meaningful Education

I've Got a College Degree, But I Can't Get a Damn Job!

While statistics have changed since the depths of the recession, a recent poll shows that many new grads and millennials move back in with their parents because they can't find a job or start a career in their field of study. You can ask almost anyone with a new grad and hear this tale of woe.

The latest Department of Labor statistics for recent grads moving back home has declined from a high of 86% to a low of 50%. However, it has not fallen for a while. In fact, while millennials are the most educated in American history, they don't seem to find much opportunity in the marketplace. They can't get a job in their field even though they have a degree.

College Grads Can't Get the Right Job

Why not?

After all, it took four, or five even six years to get a precious piece of paper that says, "I've got a degree." Many students complain that while they fulfilled the institution's requirements for a degree, they found no jobs and most discouraging, their college advisors led them to believe that, once they got their diploma, they would get a good job in their field of study! They got the degree. Now what?

Students Don't Select Majors Wisely

Just getting a degree may have been OK in the past but, with fewer well-paying jobs available today, unless the student has the right degree, he or she may have wasted those years in college.

Maybe it took five or six years because our student changed majors several times. To an extent, that is acceptable. As a famous mystery writer says, "There is always more than one story in a mystery." Often, it takes young people years to figure out their ideal career path with many mysteries in between.

Unless we are gifted, it can be difficult to know what we want to do in life. We must often check out several areas before we decide what we want to do. Later in this chapter, I include a guideline to simplify the process.

Unfortunately, many do not make smart choices and study an area that gives them few marketable skills, making it hard to start a career in that field.

Think about it. Who would hire a person with a degree from any school in an obscure topic like South Ethiopian Culture, Sumerian grammar, or Akkadian verb forms. How about the degree in Contemporary Art Expression? Almost sounds like finger painting to me.

What good are worthless majors or elective classes to the process of learning and developing skills that lead a company to pay us? The moral: Opt for a major wisely.

I saw a class at one major university called World Peace, an honorable class I'm sure, but do you think it will ever happen? You don't need a college degree to promote world peace.

PS: It won't get you credibility in your career search either.

Reality is Brutal

World Peace is an admirable and humane goal, but it's not going to happen with so much evil in the world. That doesn't mean that we shouldn't try for it, but to teach it may be just another university tactic meant to get a sizeable chunk of moola from the student.

Do you think the professor leading that class has any experience bringing World Peace to fruition? If so, where? Show me. How did they succeed?

Just ask Kofi Annan (or any of the other heads of the UN over the past 70 years). As head of the United Nations, he could not bring World Peace.

How can that professor have any credibility if they have never done it? Good intentions don't make it. Teaching theory is often subjective. Reality, is brutal.

If all you have is theory, that's a sham. Theory must be proven, even if you are an Einstein.

It's a great goal and we all pray for it, but, for the most part, it is pie in the sky! Let's get real and look at and study the classes where we are wasting our time and money.

With classes and even more brainless (at least to me) majors in our universities today, we wonder why college educations are so expensive and often ineffective. While this is a bold statement, let's look at it for a second.

A recent study revealed part of the problem: Over 36 private colleges have presidents earning over one million dollars per year, and many more are close to that.

In addition, five presidents of public colleges were paid with packages of over one million dollars with a median of over $431,000 in 2015. I believe these stats came from *U.S. News and World Report.*

What About the College Elders?

Let's face it, since college presidents spend no time in the classroom and use most of their time to raise money, our priorities are out of order.

Note: Recently while doing my research, I spoke to the President of a fine University. He stated that to keep attuned with the student body needs, he makes it a point to teach a graduate course each semester.

In talking with this University head, I asked him why other university presidents seem to have fallen away from this important function. While I'm quoting him out of context, he stated that for the most part he avoids going to the national meetings of university presidents as he finds they are only interested in talking about themselves. Yada, Yada, Yada.

Do your research when checking out schools. Find out where these presidents and department deans come from. What are you getting for your time, efforts and money?

College Administrators Are Also Out of Touch

Does this tell us why many university presidents are out of touch?

I don't know what type of classes you took while in college, but I know my college didn't offer these frivolous, wasteful, and useless classes that many colleges have added to their curricula in recent years. Not only do they add to the cost of education but do little to create a viable career path. Thank you to my parents and my guidance counselors for keeping me on track.

I was fortunate to graduate with marketable skills rather than the unmarketable skills many of today's graduates enter the workforce with. Many cannot spell (note, I've read their resumes), this after spending huge sums getting a degree! If you have ever interviewed grads with no marketable skills, you'll see what I mean. If you have ever read a letter written by a college graduate, you will be amazed at the illiteracy that abounds.

This reminds me of a story included in my book *Rekindling the American Dream*.

A recent college grad gets a job at a grocery store in the management training program. He shows up on his first day, reports to the store manager and says, "I'm ready to go. What do you want me to do?"

The store manager says, "Let's start with you sweeping the floors."

The new grad says, "But, I've got a college degree!"

The manager says, "Ah, then I'll show you how to do it."

The point is: What do we learn in schools today? This may go back further as it seems a shrinking number of the younger generation are interested in the sciences, math or engineering. Maybe this is because we place little or no emphasis on developing these skills either in high school or college. What ever happened to shop classes in high school? Going back at least 20 years, the emphasis has been on developing social curriculum.

No wonder so few young adults today know how to make tangible products, fix problems, or take a concept from idea to fruition. After all, we don't repair broken items any more, we throw them away and get new models.

With dramatic changes in today's economy, it is a plain fact that colleges are not teaching the 21st century skills we need to enter the marketplace and be snatched up and put to work. What is being taught today is often out of touch, costs too much, and does not lead to a productive career.

By my way of thinking, (note: you may discover others) here are several key reasons new grads are having employment problems. What I mean is that they are either unemployed, underemployed, or have given up and work flipping burgers.

Consider the fact the USA has lost over two and one half million jobs in the past three years and another six million people have given up on the American Dream in the past six years and are living off the government dole.

What about the three million jobs going unfilled for lack of qualified candidates? Note: most of these positions are in engineering and the sciences requiring technical skills. Here are my thoughts:

Blame (a savage word at best and I'm reluctant to use it, but I will for illustration purposes) starts with our parents work ethic. This applies to the ones that never encouraged their children to get after-school or summer jobs, but made sure the kid had a nice car, spending money they never earned, cell phones, and computers paid for by mom and dad.

Mom and Dad, it is time to give your kids a break and have them get a part time job to earn what they want. Appreciation will come later. As a second thought, focus on what classes they are taking in school. Emphasize math and the sciences where they will learn a skill and eliminate the worthless tripe. If they want to take worthless tripe classes, have them do it on their own dime! As far as parental influence goes, much can be gained by starting out with encouragement. Continue with an emphasis on doing your best, choosing the best people to hang out with, and developing expectations and responsibility.

Learn how to develop principles to live by and help them develop goals. (I know, parents, often this is difficult as we think we are already doing that, but it's worth the effort.)

While that degree is important, learning valuable information is priceless.

As Mark Twain once said, "I never let my schooling interfere with my education." School leaders, think about this: What classes in your school experience impacted your career?

I'll bet if I asked a hundred people, I would get a hundred different answers. Both high schools and colleges are a great contributor to this problem. Much less emphasis is placed on what we consider soft skills like problem solving, leadership, teamwork, and written and speaking skills, which carry a great deal of weight with employers, says a recent study by NACE, the National Association of Colleges and Employers.

If they can demonstrate skills in these areas along with a degree in a decent major, recent grads will not have to move back home even though fewer jobs are available.

Remember, opportunity comes not with a college degree but with the major selected.

Example of a Person Who Chose Wisely

Recently, I returned from a trip to Columbia, South Carolina. While I waited for our delayed flight, my wife struck up a conversation with a young lady.

She asked, "Where are you going?"

The young lady said, "France, on business."

That sparked my curiosity. "What do you do?"

"I am an International Buyer for a large multinational consumer products firm."

She seemed to be rather young for a job like that, I thought. "Where did you go to school?"

"Just graduated from the University of South Carolina. My degree is in International Consumer Purchasing."

I was curious. "Why did you choose that field?"

"When I researched colleges, I wanted a school that offered degree programs in demand by employers." (Sounded good to me.) "My research said I could expect multiple offers after graduation in International Consumer Purchasing. And guess what? I did!"

Guess it pays to do your research!

In the government and the resulting entitlement society, giving something for nothing does not create responsible beings! Tell me how giving something to someone that hasn't earned it justifies taking something from someone who has. Isn't giving something to someone of our own free will more in the American spirit?

Forgiving student loans: (Note: These loans are made on the solemn promise to repay.) No one forces you to borrow money to go to school. You are free to choose educational pursuits that don't require loans or to seek vocational or technical training that doesn't require loans.

Ninety-nine weeks of unemployment insurance and free health insurance are among the major culprits. Remember, the government cannot give what it does not take from someone else!

Earning what we get makes for responsible, forward thinking, motivated individuals.

Also, consider personal reasons you have not found a job, if you want the truth. Here it is: How about your prominent tattooed neck? Although I admit Tats are more recognized today, professional decorum is the issue. What seemed cool when you were in school, screwy facial hair, piercings, and dirty dreadlocks, may not be so cool in the business world.

Nonconformance in college may show your individuality but, since 96% of grads with decent degrees have jobs, you may want to get a mirror and face the problem.

Beards and Tattoos in The Workplace

Today is one of the most permissive times in human history to have facial hair and even tattoos. However, if you are just getting out of college and hoping to enter the corporate world, don't expect your college and corporate decorum to be the same. The cultures are different.

If you must have one or both, you will want to plan ahead. If you want a beard, think of a beard style that fits your face and is right for the position in life that you hope to enter.

To keep that beard, consider what fits best and not what is silly or trendy. As for tattoos, be discreet. They are not the same as beards and not as accepted. Same with those ear holes, okay for a jazzy bartender but not so for a banker.

Just as with beards, tats make a statement. They get read by others and don't always evoke the same interpretation. Often people look at those with a beard as either Santa or the devil, depending on who is looking. It may be the same for tats but with a different connotation.

In my many years as an executive recruiter, I never worried how candidates looked or dressed, only how good they were at their area of expertise. I figured that if they were the best, I could always get them cleaned up enough to be presentable!

Choosing Majors

Here are a few of the least attractive majors to employers if you expect to get a job to start a career path: Library Science (a notable career but bad timing in today's world of e-books and reduced funding;) and Psychology (can't get a job as most employers require a graduate degree). Clinical Psychology has a current unemployment rate of 19.5%. I suggest you research both desirable and undesirable degrees. I'm sure you will find one that fits your fancy where you can make a living. Just be sure to pick one where the graduates are in demand. Now let's go on to action recommendations:

Here is a list of the top 10 majors as listed in a 2015 Forbes article. I understand the National Association of Colleges and Employers compiled the list. The employers consist of 201 companies. Note that most are large companies stating what they want from 2016 recent grads. Listed in order:

Accounting
Computer Sciences
Finance
Business Administration- Management
Mechanical Engineering
Information Sciences and Systems
Electrical Engineering
Logistics/Supply Chain
Economics
Management Information Systems

You can also find studies on Masters Degrees as well as Doctorates. You might use this as a guideline and check it out further.

Guidelines for Parents with Students About to Enter the World of Higher Education

You may want to think about these ideas:

Find a way they can get a part-time job. Having skin in the game provides a sense of responsibility and pride.

Encourage your student get an internship along with existing classes. This is a great way to learn on the job and looks good on the resume. Large- and medium-sized companies love interns.

Take advantage of the many opportunities to do volunteer work on a regular basis. You will find plenty of good opportunities and your school can help you select the sites. Also, it looks great on the resume.

Make sure they become a regular with their guidance counselor. Most students will resist this as they are intimidated; however, it provides a method of learning what they want to do while in school and after graduation.

You will be happy to see them working on a major course of study rather than hear the old excuse of, "I'm just taking general classes and haven't selected a major yet." Last time I checked, 18 is the age of majority. With knowledge of what they are getting into, they should be able to decide on a course of study.

This also keeps them from spending extra years on their parents' dole.

Selecting a guidance counselor requires developing a game plan and having a set of questions for the guidance counselor.

They may include but are not limited to the following:

Bring a list of the student's strengths as they see them. Then ask the advisor about courses of study that best utilize these strengths.

A list of their weakest areas is also important. If we don't understand the areas we need to work on, we can never improve. For example, I don't do well with math, I'm shy around people, or I don't like to read books. Just normal items that many students may need to shore up.

You can help with that and by the way don't forget mom and dad. Most students have sloppy rooms. That doesn't mean they are slobs and doesn't count here! So, mom and dad, don't prejudge. You can prepare them to ask the advisor how they can go about improving these shortcomings. What do they like to do, what they hate to do?

The goal here is to get their advisor involved in planning and structuring their time, selecting courses to take, and helping them focus on their future.

PS: Not all or even most advisors/counselors are great at helping your student structure their time and careers.

If you end up with one just going through the motions or pushing their course of study, ask around and find the one with the best reputation who can relate and be a real advisor/counselor.

At my reunion, I met my adviser from long ago, Fr. Richard Sullivan, now in his mid-80's. He hadn't changed and is still interested in his former students and he even remembered me. Fr. Sullivan, you helped guide me and I still appreciate your candor.

Don't forget about extracurricular activities or electives. With a global economy, World History is a great way to learn about other cultures. Writing and Speech classes are great assets. In fact, they are skills that every organization is looking for in new grads. Artistry or Performing Arts classes such as theatre can enhance your poise and presentation presence. These all help create skills and friendships that last a lifetime and look good on the resume.

In my book *Rekindling the American Dream*, I devoted several of my chapters to the importance of attitude and motivation. Combine these attributes with a good education focusing on doing, learning, and thinking and you will see you and your child's dreams come true.

Part II

Continuous Self-Improvement

Food for Thought- Who Has the Remote Control?

This chapter focuses on the illusion of comparison and how it impacts you. How many of you think that young people have an issue with the comparison complex?

Everyone, based on my research.

This is where the remote control comes into play. It's like what I tell my wife, "Whoever holds the remote control has the power." When you have the control, comparison is not an issue.

Everyone remembers the time they were watching their favorite TV program when dad barged in, grabbed the remote control and tuned into the evening news.

This covers not only the TV but everything in your life. It starts young, when other people have the control over your welfare, and progresses up the ladder, from teens to as far along as middle age. While it's human nature for the most part, it can have a real negative impact if not put in its place early on.

It is the fear of not being accepted as a young person or by those at work, perhaps even among friends or acquaintances. This is when you don't have the remote in your hand.

Fear is the common denominator and fosters self-doubt. Give it no mind. Fear and self-doubt will always show up for many people, but how you cope with it will make a great difference.

People I have spoken with tell me they see only one way to handle it with success. Later in this book I have a short chapter on intimidation that covers fear.

The best way to handle fear is first be true to yourself!

Think about when you went off on your own filled with excitement only to have fear and self-doubt come to the forefront. Remember how you handled it, survived, and prospered.

I remember years ago, when our youngest daughter went to England for a year of study while in college. She left as a shy young girl and came home the next semester infused with a whole new aura of confidence and self-esteem.

She came back with the remote in her hand.

Think back to your changing point. When did you take that step that put the remote in your hand?

I would like to hear your story. I'll bet it's a great one.

Comparing Yourself with Others

Fear is also one of the biggest motivators so use it well. Keep in mind: When another person has the remote control, they have the power. Keep that remote in your hands and you will have the power over your life and welfare. We will get into this more later.

Proceeding on, think of our own comparison dilemma such as when the neighbor got a new Mercedes and we are still driving an old beater. How about the friend who has a beautiful home in an upscale neighborhood? The comparisons go on and on and we must admit we have just a bit of envy or fear.

My writing colleague John Hall, a well-known expert on career development, suggests reading the book *Don't Live Like a Millionaire* by Thomas J. Stanley, PHD and William J. Danko, PHD. This book focuses on the fact that real millionaires do not have to show off their wealth. Good example: Warren Buffett drives a 20-year-old Plymouth and lives in a house he purchased 40 years ago! Enough said.

We all realize that envy and fear are two of the seven deadly sins, but the problem goes beyond that. Look what it can do not only to young adults as well but to us.

Here's an example: A teen hangs around a gang in high school because it's cool to do. If it's the wrong type of gang it can end with that teen in jail, hooked on drugs because the rest of the guys do it, or even killed because they wanted to be cool!

Influence can have a huge impact on self-esteem and the way they see themselves.

Recent current events in Baltimore, Ferguson, etc. show how young people as well as adults can have a drastic impact on lives by following the crowd, giving the remote to others.

Here is another perspective on the fallacy of being a victim of the police and the excuses that go with it.

Over the past couple of years, much ado has been made by certain elements that the police are profiling groups, making them victims. I'll ask only one question, do you think even one police officer has ever woke up in the morning, kissed their wife and kids goodbye and said, "Now I'm going out and kill somebody!"

I don't think so. I believe they are like everyone else, they want to do their job and go home at night safe and sound.

Here is example of following the crowd. Recently I had dinner with a police officer colleague of Rob, my son-in-law. The officer's name is Martin. While talking about gangs and their influence on youths Martin told me the story of a childhood incident.

Martin had grown up in a high crime and violence gang neighborhood. While he never joined a gang, he had to find a way to survive. He did this by keeping his distance yet not creating enemies. One day his friends, also non-gang members, decided they wanted to have fun by chasing girls, a natural boy/girl game. Instead of participating, Martin decided he wanted to see a popular movie of the time, *Jurassic Park*. He chose well that day and went to the movie.

His friends should have made a similar choice as a few of the girls they were wooing were part of a local gang. Suddenly, while they were doing their boyish pranks, a drive-by shooter in a car raked Martin's friends with bullets from an AK47. The result? Dead and wounded young boys. Martin made the right choice or got lucky that fateful day. We make choices like this every day.

Here is a short story about choices and luck.

It is said Admiral Chester Nimitz, Commander of the American naval forces in the Pacific during the Battle of Midway in World War Il, made a famous remark at the end of the battle. This battle took place in mid-1942, a few months after the Japanese dismantled the American Naval Fleet at Pearl Harbor. The Japanese Navy, at its peak and all powerful with combat experienced leadership, had a huge naval fleet.

However, the American navy, while smaller, undermanned, and beat up, destroyed the Japanese fleet and changed WWII in the Pacific. Nimitz later asked, "Were we better or just lucky?" We will never know the answer for certain, but we do know that some choices are good, some are less than good, and some are just lucky.

As young people, we can only hope we make choices that don't have a negative impact on our lives. As we get older we either can get smarter or you know the others! Yes, dumber or go on making the same stupid choices.

Maybe his friends were in the wrong place at the wrong time. Perhaps Martin made the right choice that day or got lucky. Now he is not only a respected police officer helping others to make good decisions, he is one of the best officers on the force.

Being aware of your choices and not following the crowd can influence how lucky you are.

Ask yourself what questions can influence your life? Am I too fat, too thin, am I too smart, am I too dumb, too ugly, too pretty, too lazy, too ambitious, too well educated, not educated enough, should have gone to a better school, too rich, or too poor? Do I hang out with the right people?

If we are enthralled by the comparison complex, we might always be asking am I too... or should I have. . .? As a result- how can we ever expect to realize our true potential if we compare ourselves with others? If we ask these types of questions or tell the younger set that they should have, chances are they will forever suffer from this envy complex. Think about it! Maybe you can give them the remote at some point. You and they may be surprised. Please don't tell my wife. I'm not about to give up the remote or the power.

Here are a few ideas to keep the control in your hand:

Be true to yourself: What do you want out of life? What is important to you? Don't worry about the answer as the importance may change over time. Be careful of who you hang with. They will influence your life.

Remember, you are special and unique. Don't worry about comparison. It is an illusion.

Choices: Do the right thing. You will seldom go wrong. Note: you may, but, in my opinion, you will hold yourself responsible.

Set goals and figure out what to do to achieve them

Write them down and keep track. Add to and subtract from them over time.

Intimidation and Fear

Have you heard fear and intimidation are an illusion?

It is not unusual for just about everyone at one time or another to experience that illusion. Intimidation and fear are also a hindrance to success. It is a natural emotion. Now if only we could channel that emotion and turn the same energy into confidence, we would be very powerful and wonderful things will happen. This does not mean overconfidence or arrogance, just plain confidence.

Years ago, Eleanor Roosevelt (if you don't know who she is, Google her) talked about this in her book. She recounted her first dance with her future President and husband Franklin. He so intimidated her that she constantly stepped on his toes. Franklin, being a gentleman, sensed she might be frightened of him.

He told her to relax. "I won't bite," he said.

Years later after the war, after her appointment as a United Nations envoy, she traveled overseas with her shy youngest grandson. Along the way, she sensed all the world leaders intimidated him so she told him the story of her first dance with his grandfather. "Just be yourself," she told him. That made the difference. He blossomed during the rest of the trip.

Actress Susan Jefferies handles fear and intimidation this way, "Feel the fear and just do it."

Joe Namath, Hall of fame quarterback of the New York Jets, and Jerry West of Los Angeles Laker fame both tell similar stories. Before every game their fear of not performing up to the level of expectations would create trauma. Both would be so intimidated with this fear that they would vomit in the locker room before every game. Intimidation and fear can be debilitating if unchecked.

Since they both became members of the Hall of Fame, it is obvious they could re-channel this fear into confidence and succeed at the highest level.

One of my colleagues, Kay Vickery, thought a good ending to this chapter might be to list a few ideas on how to overcome these bad illusions and re-channel our fears into confidence so here are a few:

Talking with the people that tend to intimidate you will dissipate their power over you. The more you get to talk with them, the more you will be on equal footing. Confidence will ensue.

Make a good impression. Show up on time, dress, speak and act professional, no matter what. The intimidator will be impressed. Be prepared, speak with clarity, and don't ramble. Preparation overcomes fear.

Ask questions, for example, as simple as: Tell me about yourself. Where are you from, do you have a family? What do you like to do? Simple, non-intimidating questions make for good conversation openers.

Getting people to talk about themselves will go a long way to clear the mystery. You never know, you may even have a mutual interest

Make a list of things you have done that you are proud of, be prepared for the follow up questions such as, how did you do that? Knowing you are good brings confidence. Suggestion: Start with the present and go backwards. Take a deep breath and let it out slowly. Calmness takes over. Listen first, sell second, you will be surprised how well that method works when you are trying to get a point across.

Consider the three questions a good salesman uses to get to know their new customer 1) What are you doing now? 2) What do you like about it? 3) What changes would you like to see happen? They are simple and easy to answer yet provide a wealth of information.

Our fears often appear perilous. This is the extreme. The situation is not as perilous as we have convinced ourselves. Use the middle ground of prudence as your guideline.

In your conversation, make it a dialog not a monologue.

Remember President Roosevelt's advice, they too won't bite.

Speaking in Public

Public speaking is like this for many: The fear of making a public speech often makes people so sick they cannot go through with it. If they do, they make a fool of themselves.

Yes, it can be debilitating even if it is an illusion.

It is a shame that many qualified individuals would rather lick the bottom of their shoes than give a speech or make a presentation to a group.

Being with Toastmasters for many years now, I have seen this (and experienced it myself I may add), especially for the inexperienced. In Toastmasters, the goal is to not only help participants become better speakers but to get those butterflies to fly in formation. It works. This is a great organization for all.

Even the most experienced public speakers feel those butterflies before every public outing. By making the butterflies work to their advantage, that adrenalin comes to good use.

This goes for those starting a new job, meeting with a person who may be important to their career, or teeing off on the first hole in the club championship.

What can we do to help us re-channel our fears and intimidation into confidence?

Here are a few thoughts:

First, develop confidence in your own innate ability. This does not mean flying by the seat of your pants. You must work and prepare to be exceptional. Mel Bartholomew, visionary, inventor of Square Foot Gardening and author of the largest selling gardening book, suggests a way to improve your skills. Before making a presentation, get a tape recorder or use your smart phone app and record the first five minutes.

Then listen to it. You will hear how you sound to others, you will then know if you need to work more on that opening. Mel's method provides a means to make you more comfortable and proficient by acing the opening, getting you off to a good start. As I say later, in baseball for a pitcher strike one counts! One idea I like to suggest for new speakers is to keep in mind that your audience is here to learn from what you say. You are the teacher.

The audience wants to be on your side. They are your friend. Give them good, meaningful information in a well-prepared and thought-out manner. This takes preparation and practice.

Believe in yourself, and trust your ability, and never let them see you sweat! We all screw up so get over it and get on with it.

The next part of this chapter involves stories of people that have pulled themselves up by the bootstraps, over-coming the obvious handicaps of being poor, not smart enough, not tall enough, coming from the wrong side of the tracks, or just not pretty or handsome enough. They may have even got hooked in with the wrong crowds. The goal is to show you that spirit, attitude, motivation, and being yourself are the prime things that count.

Part III

Success Story Updates

The Story of Officer Robert Pedregon

Here is an update from *Rekindling the American Dream*. It is the story of Robert Pedregon and his first night out as a police officer of the noted LAPD LAX division known as the World Police.

Since that time many changes have occurred. Along with being promoted three times from then till now, he is now a "111," a member of the prestigious LAPD Honor Guard, a Distinguished Expert Marksman (note: of which very few are awarded), has been used as a model on World Police recruiting promotions, entered and passed the Motor Academy, so he is now a Motor cop at LAX, has a high arrest and conviction ratio and has received the prestigious *Governor's Medal of Valor Award* from the State's Governor and State Attorney General for going above and beyond the CALL OF DUTY in an event at LAX. Likewise, he received the Medal of Valor from the California Peace Officers Association.

Here's the story and how I understand it happened:

November 1, 2013 began as a beautiful morning in Los Angeles, a place of beauty on days like this. One problem: Evil people can turn beauty into ugliness and destroy others' lives, hopes, and dreams with one evil act. Our hero Rob, on morning duty in his patrol car, was driving down Century Blvd., near the Airport. Then his radio came alive. Shooting at terminal 3! No other information available! He spun his vehicle around and raced to terminal 3.

Within 38 seconds he exited and ran to the terminal entrance. Still no info available, only a bunch of passengers panicking and yelling out. By then, a few more officers arrived. Without much to go on, they assembled and fortunately they had trained the prior two weeks for such a happening.

The lead sergeant, Rob and three other officers took pursuit. Passengers were fleeing one way. They went the other way, toward the danger. They walked in a diamond formation with one in front (the lead), one in back to cover the rear and one on each side to cover the flanks. Rob took the right wing. They found the dead TSA Agent, the wounded passenger, and a deserted terminal. Note: later they found a few hiders. Still, they had little info on the number of shooters or where they were, just a few scattered reports from panicked passenger cell phones. They did know the shots were coming from an automatic high-powered rifle. They were outgunned, not a good thing. Proceeding per department tactics without regards to their personal safety and hearing activity, they forged ahead until the first shots came at them.

Winston Churchill once said nothing is as exhilarating as having shots fired at you ... and missing.

Now they at least knew the location of one of the shooters and none of them had been hit yet, even though he fired bursts of automatic fire with many near misses. Later the FBI told Rob one of the shooter's bullets missed his right temple by less than an inch.

Now it's time to take him down.

And here is where Police training comes into play. They had a plan and executed it to perfection. Under the plan, the lead sergeant would take the first shots with Rob at his flank. With exposure at a minimum, the sergeant executed it to perfection and took him down.

On command and without regard to his personal safety, Rob raced forward, kicked the gun from the killer's arm, assessed the damage, and calmly faced the shooter, eye to eye. As he secured the killer, he noticed the man was bleeding out. They couldn't do much as they still didn't know if other shooters were around, but, as good officers, they did their duty and saved the dirty rotten evil SOB.

All the excitement was over. It all happened in less than four minutes, 38 seconds for Rob to reach the scene and less than three minutes to gather the squad, plan and execute it to perfection.

Training, presence, confidence in team and system saved many lives that fateful day.

Later officers discovered the scumbag shooter had a note reading: Kill TSA and the PIGS! I have met his teammates and had nice conversations with the lead sergeant. He told me how proud and honored he was to have Rob at his side that day. He couldn't stop issuing his praises of how Rob acted under the highest of pressure and would be glad to have Rob at his 6 (back) under any circumstance. This from a man that served in combat in the military as well as a gang sergeant with LAPD, where he experienced gunfights.

I asked him how he coped with the shooting. He told me he had problems. I told him he and his team are in my prayers every day. Thank God for these brave men that risk their lives every day to save our sorry souls.

That's our update on Police Officer 111 Motors Unit, Los Angeles World Police Robert Pedregon. I asked my daughter Nicole, yes Rob is my son-in-law, how she handles what he does every day. She said, "He chose a life of service..."

Breaking News: I just learned Robert has made another move. Even though he is not yet a Sergeant, he has been put on loan to be the head of public relations (PIO) for Chief of Police Gannon for the next seven months. What an honor!

Oh, just received word another honor has been bestowed on our brave cop.

Dateline Chicago October 2015: Secretary General of InterPort Police and Chair of 9/11 Award Committee on terrorism has awarded Officer Robert Pedregon the 2015 Medal of Heroism and Valor! My gosh, guess I'll have to be more respectful to my son-in-law!

Rob followed his dream and brought honor to his family, friends, his team and fellow Officers, the city, on and on.

With all the recent shooting of cops and first responders I think of the saying, "These colors (blue) don't run."

In the military, they say when pinning a medal on a soldier for bravery, "He stood up and was counted..." Indeed!

This is not easy, but, if we are to succeed, consider Rob's example and follow your dreams.

The Day I Almost Quit Being a Police Officer

A Master Gardener colleague, Ed Andrade, who retired after 35 years as a police officer in Santa Ana, CA, told me this story of doing the right thing and caring.

Santa Ana has a large Latino population with a huge gang problem. Earlier in this book, I included a story about a young man in Santa Ana who opted out of gang activity. Making the right choice had a great impact on his life.

Ed told this story to his daughter when she considered becoming a police officer. He wanted her to understand the good as well as bad in making this career choice.

Ed's story went like this. He had just returned from a three-day training class at the Marine base at Camp Pendleton near San Diego. The class focused on Swat team procedures. At the time, Ed, a sergeant, headed up a Santa Ana police Swat Team.

After intense training, the department assigned his team to a downtown substation where crime and violence were a way of life. One Friday night, rather than wait for a call in the station, Ed decided to walk the street to visit with the citizens. He figured by mixing in they would see his presence and get to know the police were looking out for them.

The downtown neighborhood had about twenty bars, some nice and some not so nice. Ed's routine was to stop in the bar and talk to the bartenders and the patrons on an informal basis and go on to the next stop. After visiting a few, his next visit turned nasty. He walked in, exchanged greetings and as he turned one of the patrons for no known reason wound up and slugged him in the face, breaking his nose and inflicting facial damage.

Rather than fight in the bar, Ed took the fight outside where they went at it. Both got in good shots. The instigator went after Ed's gun and it got nastier.

Now the crowd chose sides and Ed lost, not the fight but the crowd. All around him he heard the crowd shouting, "Kill the cop, kill the cop." This gathered momentum.

In the meantime, the bad guy went after Ed's gun. He failed and after four or five minutes Ed got him down and handcuffed.

When interviewed later and asked why he did it, the thug said, "I hate cops!" When Ed got home that night he reflected on what had happened. He couldn't get over the crowds "kill the cop" and the "I hate cops" rhetoric.

As a police officer for all those years, dedicating his life to serving his city and protecting the public, this disheartened him. Ed said for the next week he couldn't go back to work as he contemplated his future. By the end of that week, he realized he chose this profession so he could defend his community and its citizens. After all, if he didn't who would? He continued his chosen mission.

From here on these are my own comments so, take them as you may Whether it be a policeman, firefighter, soldier, teacher or others that help keep us safe and help mold our American values a simple thank you will go a long way. God Bless them.

Update on the Story of Greg Edwards

Now for an update on our third story from *Rekindling the American Dream*, the story of Greg Edwards.

When we left off Greg had lost his Buffalo, NY based business in 2006. Large embroidery company with 50 employees... out of business. He could have given up, but he didn't. Within six weeks he joined a 2-Billion-dollar company in Philadelphia and within a few years became their salesman of the year. A few years later, he was promoted to National VP of Sales.

Greg is a go-getter and put all his effort into his career. It worked out well, which is not a surprise.

In 2013 a former colleague and investor asked Greg if he wanted to once again go out on his own. They decided to purchase a healthcare focused valet parking company.

Greg saw that due to Obamacare and the aging population, hospitals all around the US were getting busier and busier. They were running out of convenient parking for their patients, visitors and guests. Valet parking, done right, was a huge patient satisfaction tool.

The new partnership worked well with Greg as the rainmaker and his partner as the financial guy.

Eighteen months later, their company is doing over $5 million in revenue, twice the size of Greg's first company in Buffalo. They now have customers from California to Florida and Texas to Minnesota.

The old saying of "Most overnight successes take a few years" is so true. Greg has spent the last 10 years in the outsourcing of services to healthcare space. His knowledge and contacts are the reason he first saw the opportunity and second was then able to make it into a viable business. Long hours and hard work helped too.

This may seem like an amazing tale of luck and being in the right place at the right time, but you have to know Greg Edwards. Greg has always had a make-it-happen mentality along with passion, determination and a never-give-up attitude. His favorite saying is, "The harder I work, the luckier I get."

His latest focus is hospital gift shops. As he put it, a completely untapped market!

More to follow with this guy!

Another Update: The Doc and The Girl

Here is another update on the three stories from *Rekindling the American Dream*. This is three years later. So how are they doing?

Our second update is the story of *The Doc and the Girl*. You will recall they moved from Los Angeles to Columbia, SC after graduating and finding it difficult to find a job that fit their degrees in California, the land of milk and honey.

He had a Doctorate in Chiropractic Medicine, she a Masters in film production.

Sounds like it would be easy to get situated. However, it was not easy and, while he had his Doctorate, as a new chiropractor he had no following.

We were also in the middle of the greatest recession since 1929 and both employment and workman's compensation were way down. That chiropractors did much of their business based on workplace injuries made it hard to get started.

He soon joined a fine practice, but they could only keep him busy two days per week.

The rest of the time, to make a living he had to work as a handyman.

This is when he decided to look for chiropractic opportunities in other states. He found one in Columbia, SC. He and the "girl" took the big step and he accepted the chiropractic position in Columbia.

At this point he is running a Chiropractic practice in Columbia and is in the process of purchasing a practice in of all places Austin, TX. He has been with the same practice for six years and has grown it each year. He is well respected in the community.

The girl had her Masters in film production and started at Paramount Studios in a junior position as a Studio Tour Guide. Along the way, she received several promotions. Only problem: They stopped making movies in California and, while the studios respected her ability, prospects were nil. When they moved, she gave up her job at Paramount and left for South Carolina with no position in sight. After they arrived, she heard about an opening at the FOX Television Station in Columbia and applied. (Networking pays) They hired her. Believe me, it was not the position for a person with a Master's degree.

She has now been with FOX Television for five years. During that time, she has been promoted several times and taken on new responsibilities with each move up. She loves what she does.

Breaking news: I learned she just received the *Leadership Award* among a group of manager types taking the Dale Carnegie Leadership Course. Before this I asked for her comments for my upcoming chapter on prima donnas and essential incompetents. A good deal of that chapter is based on her comments along with others.

Just goes to show you what two people can do when the opportunities arise, especially when you graduate and find nothing fits what you expected. Almost like making the best out of a bad situation. If you are fortunate to live a long life, this won't be the worst situation that comes your way.

If this fits your situation, find what works for you no matter where it begins. You must control how it continues, so keep the remote in your hands.

Part IV

Leadership and Mentorship

Transforming Your Life

Having a meaningful, successful, happy life requires a constant regimen of finding ways and methods to keep up with the world. This may require making small changes all the time. These small changes can only help improve your life but also your outlook. They enable us to keep from being out of touch and thus are meaningful. When we become too lazy or satisfied, being out of touch is near.

For example, learn how to effectively use your computer. For many more mature people it's a mystery that causes frustration and even loss of self-confidence. Younger people have grown up with technology and it seems natural, so they don't have that problem. Many Junior Colleges or other organizations (like SCORE) have free or almost free classes where we can get good tutorials on computers and social media that will make this mystery go away. No matter what age we are, learning is still within our ability.

Put that mystery on your Bucket List and see for yourself. Then watch your confidence soar.

Think back even 10 years. What issues did we face then? Unemployment or underemployment were not issues, but the Iraq war was. Fortunately, since then we first won that war then, unfortunately, we lost it again.

Now our issues are different and employment and underemployment has raised its ugly head with almost fifty million Americans on government assistance and over eighty million Americans giving up getting a job or are way underemployed.

Have we seen any changes in technology and social media? You bet.

Then we have the controversy over global warming and man's influence on it and how about the racial divide and the degradation of law enforcement. And we haven't even talked about the numerous government scandals, lost e-mails, Benghazi, fast and furious, the Mideast, the entitlement society, health care, immigration and the progressives move toward socialism. Personal note: Where has this ever worked?

Many more exist, like student loans and lower average family incomes, but let's go on.

While I have my opinions, we will not discuss these issues now. For the most part, they are above my pay grade and are just that, my opinion. However, we can control our lives and make the best of it.

Now we don't have to devote a big portion of our time and energy to these endeavors, just a little bit on how we can Unbridle the American Spirit.

This reminds me of a story told by a friend of mine. He is an extraordinary fellow by the name of Murray Schrantz. Murray is a West Point grad, ex-Ranger and co-author of our book *Adapt or Perish*. He is also a member of our business and communications group.

He is a giver and spends most of his time helping veterans get placed in meaningful jobs after they leave the military. This has been a frustrating but rewarding goal. It seems in this country we have many well-qualified vets, but a segment of them were injured in combat operations and have difficulty finding jobs. The problem seems to be that most companies are not interested in hiring these disabled vets as they can be difficult to adapt back into civilian society. His mission has been to not change the disabled but to teach a company how to work with these capable individuals. This is notable. Thank you, Murray, a meaningful endeavor!

Touching others makes for a meaningful life. I have more to come on this subject.

In your case, put a plan in place that will work the best for all your life. I hope it will give you new energy and keep you on top all your life.

Here are a few suggestions from people that I have respected and admired over many years. Hope they are as beneficial to you as they have been to me.

Continuing Education Thoughts

How do we continue having a meaningful life? One way is to utilize continuing education and reading good self-help books.

Let's start with good books. Research has found that reading good self-help books by experts in a field will lead to greater knowledge in that area. Might be a book on leadership, writing, or maybe gardening (one of my personal interests), depends on your preference.

Try to get on a regular program where you read one per month. If you only get one idea from each book you read, you will be way ahead. One good self-help book per year is good, six per year is better, twelve per year is best. Libraries have them for free on loan, e-books are rather inexpensive, used book stores are cheap, and paperback books a bit more expensive but worth the price. Do your research and you are on your way. Good luck.

As far as continuing education goes, if you plan on advancing in your career, a continuous education program will keep you in a forever learning mode. Many young people think that once they have their degree that part of their education is complete. Yes, they say, "No more school for me!"

In my way of thinking, we learn all our years and having a bit of experience helps. Now is the time to get good.

Take classes on a regular basis to improve those areas that will impact your future.

Remember, you are never too old to learn.

Oh, and don't forget to take classes from time to time that are fun. With online classes from major universities, it's easy to fit in the time while you are working.

A Few More Things to Consider

Attitude, motivation and spirit will supersede and overcome pure brilliance or brains. Of course, having all of them is priceless. However, not all of us have all, maybe just a few of these attributes.

Like anything else, we can work on improving and if we do we will improve. Suggestion: Start now! Why? We are all born with different traits both plus and minus. Our goal is to hone our strong traits and improve our weaker areas in order that we become the best self we can be.

As a Master Gardener, I've always enjoyed teaching young children gardening basics, especially growing edibles.

Since our economy has evolved from agrarian to industrial, kids today often have no idea where their food comes from.

When asked, their only thought is it comes from the local supermarket.

Parents often come to me amazed that suddenly their kids want to eat the vegetables they grew in our school garden. They witnessed how, starting as a seed, with a little care the plant morphed into a tasty, healthful food item, whereas before it was more than a chore to get them to eat their vegetables.

The point is that today's kids and maybe a good majority of our young adults don't seem to know what it takes to make, fix or grow something.

When they find out, their perspective changes. Guess much of this may be due to today's "Big Box" disposable society syndrome that kills a child's natural curiosity. Just toss it and buy a newer, better device or go to the store and buy more food.

For me, when they find out how to grow, fix or make, they value the knowledge this brings with the result that they become curious. Curiosity is good!

They ask questions and figure it out for themselves, rather than take your word for it.

A whole lot different than the typical answer: Eat your vegetables because they are good for you.

This philosophy can work in all aspects of life. For example, it intrigues me that a company that develops and makes or delivers a product that improves our quality of life can often be denigrated by one side of our society for making a profit. Without profit, the company could not invest in research to develop new products, create new jobs, get investors or pay salaries. After all, controlling costs is a basis of economics 101.

Competition, then determines product price, viability, and higher wages.

Perhaps our schools should add basic economics to their curriculum. Maybe we should also get back to those old Home Economics and Shop classes.

Not all of us by nature are meant to be doctors, lawyers, engineers, or scientists. What we do not want to be is a burden on our fellow human beings.

We can do a lot of good and be great people by just striving to be our best. Parents can be a great influence by instilling values, not by trying to be an undue aberration on their children. A good value system can make for a happy, productive life. Okay, enough. I encourage you to think about it and remember to keep the remote in your hand.

How Do We Decide?

When it comes to what we should do, here is a good technique learned a long time ago. It has always been an influence in my decision making. It's called The Ben Franklin Method. It seems that Ole Ben had a system when faced with a decision. He would take a piece of paper and make a line down the middle. At the top left, he would write "good" and on the other side "bad." Starting with the good, he would begin listing the good. Then, on the other side, he would list the bad. When completed, the answer became very apparent.

The same system can be used by making different column headings such as; pro/con, good/evil, buy/not buy, go to this school or that school. Try it out, I think you will like it.

Maybe you heard about the 104-year-old woman being interviewed by the local newspaper on her secrets for living a long life. When the reporter asked her, "What is the best thing about being 104?" She replied," No peer pressure!"

Peer pressure is an inane entity. It can push us to be the very best we can be or it can cause us to be the very least.

Here are a few of my thoughts that can help:

Be a bright light in your activities.

Look on the sunny side and be thankful for what you do. As someone said, as humble as it may be, you don't have to have the biggest house or car to show off.

Success comes twice, first in our mind and then in our body by our actions. Think about it, then do it!

What if we make a stupid decision? That is, one that we later regretted. Don't worry. We all do. We speak in the heat of the time or act on gut instincts that backfire.

Haven't we all done that? It would not be human if all our words and actions were perfect. Get on with it (like my old coach said) and take the good with the bad. Be sure to learn as you go. Be wary to criticize and easy to forgive.

Making good decisions can be a start to a successful, happy life. Keep working on it all your life.

History of The Car Radio

Here's one more story that I thought you might like. Since this book is about how we can unleash our ingenuity, this story caught my attention when a friend, Vern Davis, put me on to it. Since I had not heard it before, you may not have either. While it's not about Bill Gates or Steve Jobs, it goes back in history a bit to show how history and our quality of life has been impacted by innovation.

Seems like cars have always had radios, but they didn't. Here's the true story:

One evening in 1929, two young men named William Lear and Elmer Wavering drove their girlfriends to a lookout point high above the Mississippi River town of Quincy, Illinois to watch the sunset.

It was a romantic night to be sure, but one of the women observed that it would be even nicer if they could listen to music in the car. Lear and Wavering liked the idea.

Both men had tinkered with radios (Lear had served as a radio operator in the U.S. Navy during World War I) and before long they took apart a home radio and tried to get it to work in a car. Not as easy as it sounds. Automobiles have ignition switches, generators, spark plugs, and other electrical equipment that generate noisy static interference, making it impossible to listen to the radio with the engine running.

One by one, Lear and Wavering identified and eliminated each source of electrical interference. When they got their radio to work, they took it to a radio convention in Chicago, where they met Paul Galvin, owner of Galvin Manufacturing Corporation.

He made a product called a battery eliminator, a device that allowed battery-powered radios to run on household AC current. But, as more homes were wired for electricity, more radio manufacturers made AC-powered radios. Galvin needed a new product to manufacture. When he met Lear and Wavering, he found it. He believed that mass-produced, affordable car radios had the potential to become a huge business.

Lear and Wavering set up shop in Galvin's factory, and when they perfected their first radio, they installed it in his Studebaker. Then Galvin went to a local banker to apply for a loan. Thinking it might sweeten the deal, he had his men install a radio in the banker's Packard. Good idea but it didn't work. Half an hour after the installation, the banker's Packard caught fire. (They didn't get the loan.)

Galvin didn't give up. He drove his Studebaker 800 miles to Atlantic City to show off the radio at the 1930 Radio Manufacturers Association convention. Too broke to afford a booth, he parked the car outside the convention hall and cranked up the radio so that passing conventioneers could hear it. That idea worked. He got enough orders to put the radio into production.

What's in a Name?

They called the first production model the 5 T71. Galvin decided he needed to come up with a little catchier name. In those days, many companies in the phonograph and radio business used the suffix "Ola" for their names. Radiola, Columbiola, and Victrola were three of the biggest. Galvin decided to do the same, and since he intended his radio for use in a motor vehicle, he decided to call it Motorola.

But, even with the name change, the radio still had problems.

When the Motorola went on sale in 1930, it cost about $110 uninstalled at a time when you could buy a brand-new car for $650. The country was also sliding into the Great Depression. (By that calculation, a radio for a new car would cost about $3,000 today.) In 1930 it took two men several days to put in a car radio. The dashboard had to be taken apart so that the receiver and a single speaker could be installed, and the ceiling had to be cut open to install the antenna. These early radios ran on their own batteries, not on the car battery, so holes had to be cut into the floorboard to accommodate them.

The installation manual had eight complete diagrams and 28 pages of instructions. Selling complicated car radios that cost 20 percent of the price of a brand-new car wouldn't have been easy in the best of times, let alone during the Great Depression.

Galvin lost money in 1930 and struggled for a couple of years. In 1933, when the economy picked up, Ford began to offer Motorola radios pre-installed at the factory. In 1934 they got another boost when Galvin struck a deal with B.F. Goodrich to sell and install them in its chain of tire stores. By then the price of the radio, installation included, had dropped to $55. The Motorola car radio took off. The official name of the company would change from Galvin Manufacturing to Motorola in 1947.

In the meantime, Galvin continued to develop new uses for car radios. In 1936, the same year that it introduced push-button tuning, it also introduced the Motorola Police Cruiser, a standard car radio factory preset to a single frequency to pick up police broadcasts. In 1940, he developed the first handheld two-way radio, the Handie-Talkie, for the U.S. Army. A lot of communications technologies that we take for granted today were born in Motorola labs in the years that followed World War II. In 1947 they came out with the first television to sell under $200. In 1956 the company introduced the world's first pager. In 1969 it supplied the radio and television equipment used to televise Neil Armstrong's first steps on the Moon. In 1973 it invented the world's first handheld cellular phone. Motorola is one of the largest cell phone manufacturers in the world. And it all started with the car radio.

Whatever happened to the two men who installed the first radio in Paul Galvin's car?

Elmer Wavering and William Lear ended up taking very different paths in life. Wavering stayed with Motorola. In the 1950's he helped change the automobile experience again when he developed the first automotive alternator, replacing inefficient, unreliable generators. The invention lead to such luxuries as power windows, power seats, and, later, air-conditioning.

Lear also continued inventing. He holds more than 150 patents. Remember the eight-track tape players? Lear invented that.

However, what he's most famous for are his contributions to the field of aviation. He invented radio direction finders for planes and aided in the invention of the auto-pilot. He also designed the first automatic aircraft landing system. In 1963, he introduced his most famous invention, the Lear Jet, world's first mass-produced, affordable business jet. Not bad for a guy who dropped out of school after the eighth grade.

It is fun to find out how the many conveniences that we take for granted came into being!

And it all started with a woman's suggestion!

Back in the mid 70's I worked for a division of Motorola, but, to tell you the truth, I never heard this story. It couldn't work that way today. Yet how did Microsoft, Apple and even Hewlett-Packard get started? You're right! Someone had an idea and acted on it.

Making Life Matter - A Cake of Yeast

This is a side note. Have you ever wondered if your life matters? No, I mean really matters. Not just to you but to the people around you, family, friends, your country or even the world.

I don't know about you, but I think about this a lot. Most of the time, it's when I sit down to write like I'm doing now.

As I begin to ponder, I often think, "Why am I doing this? Or will it make any difference? Even more important, will anyone read it or, what will they think? Will they give it any credibility? Even, should they? - After all who am I, what have I done to deserve their credulity?"

It's almost like a cake of yeast. I recently read a book by Fr. Jonathan Morris, called *Light in the Darkness*. (Great book, by the way) Fr. Morris spoke about how magical a cake of yeast can be. Imagine how when you add a cake of yeast, the dough transcends into a new form, almost magical.

This can happen with you when you inject your influence into others in ways you cannot imagine. It can impact or change a life.

Here is an illustration. As I write this I got an Instagram picture and message from Austin Pedregon (Rob Pedregon's son). When he visited the State Capitol in Sacramento, he saw a picture of his father receiving the Medal of Valor on prominent display in the Capital building. Can you imagine what this meant to a son? Can you imagine seeing a picture of a loved one being honored for their valor?

Now this is an anomaly as we don't have to be a recognized hero to make a difference in a life.

It's as simple as giving hope to others by what you say and do. At times, it's just by listening or giving encouragement when they need it most or helping others.

Maybe we influence our children by our life actions, even by our writings, actions or the way we conduct our everyday life, maybe just a personal note on a greeting card.

As I consider these matters, it comes back to the fact that it's not me that matters; it's the person reading my ruminations that matters. After all, maybe they can get new ideas out of what other people have shared with me.

The answer is: Yes, your life matters, especially if you influence other people's lives.

How you do that is up to you.

Also, it helps me when you buy my books. Oops, did I just say that? Thanks anyway, and don't forget you can influence a lot of people by just influencing one!

Are You a Prima Donna or Essential Incompetent?

Sounds like an oxymoron if you are or aren't and have to deal with either or both. But, is it? Very few ever discuss either one so let's spend time on these two personal traits. Most often they are only spoken about in terms of personal transgression, such as that idiot thinks she is a prima donna or that person can't do anything right!

First let's define what I mean by both.

Prima Donna: A person with a huge ego (sometimes deserved and sometimes not).

These folks are often high achievers, well-motivated, confident, high energy, high-profile driven types who often need special handling. They are used to getting their own way and don't like to acquiesce to others, especially others that are considered on a lesser rung of the ladder. Now this is not all bad. The way to consider the high achiever types is like a greyhound racing dog. Those that love them or are their trainers realize that to get the best results they need special treatment.

As managers, we need to realize this and treat them accordingly if we want to realize their potential for our purposes and theirs. Almost like dealing with a diva. Treat them well and they will sing a great aria.

Essential Incompetents

Essential Incompetents: I don't know if a real definition exists, but here is the way I look at it in two simple words, useful idiots. (Note: this is what Lenin called them.)

They are an essential part of a team. They may be new on the job or are responsible for an area that is essential to team success. They even may be veteran members of the team. Only problem is they are incompetent or don't do their job as expected. Most of the time they need to be either taught, straightened out, or if they don't get it they don't have a job.

As an example, think of a chef at a restaurant. While they can prepare the food, they can't run the restaurant by themselves. They need others like waiters, busboys, dishwashers and others. All of them become an essential part of the team and success is dependent on how each performs. Thus, if one of them does not give a consistent performance, they may be considered an essential incompetent. Got it? Let's move on.

I've been doing research on this subject and realized that, in every organization I've ever been involved with, I've had to deal with countless numbers of both prima donnas and essential incompetents on athletic teams, at schools, business or nonprofit organizations, and even in the companies we worked with or for.

Now, I can't take myself out of the mix as from time to time, I've been both. In fact, if you speak to my wife now, she would might say yes, he is both, right now! Maybe I better get straightened out.

So, as we get into this discussion, don't exclude yourself from the issue on either side.

I have never come across anyone discussing these subjects in an open forum and I don't know if any studies on prima donnas or essential incompetents exist.

Most of the time, they are discussed around the water fountain, over drinks, or a small gettogether where the main topics are talking behind others backs! Let's face it. Nothing good ever comes out of these back-stabbing events.

It's interesting how I got hooked on the subject and started my research by asking people I know about the subject.

Most people I spoke to didn't understand my point, most just thought, "Oh, well, it's all a part of working with others." To me it was obvious they had never given it much thought. Here is what got me started.

A senior manager I know was talking about a person he had just promoted. The company is a high-profile media company and has plenty of both prima donnas and essential incompetents.

When questioned, he said one of the key qualities of the person he promoted was she knew how to deal with both and get the results she needed.

Most important, she not only got the results in the time frame required but also got the culprit to want to fulfill her needs.

Let's start out with essentials that have incompetent habits. For example, I'm reminded of a great police officer that is reluctant or consistently late in filling out casework or gets their partner to do it, even gets their partner to explain the case to the sergeant or lieutenant because they are not good or confident in writing or making oral presentations. Otherwise, they are great. The result? They never get promoted no matter how good they are in other areas.

I'm reminded of a recent article from Bill Marriott of Marriott Hotels, who stressed that his future managers are trained to be good in all areas as this is essential for team success. He is proud that 65% of Marriott's senior managers started in the lowest positions in their hotels. This is a tribute to a training program that focuses on both essential incompetents and prima donnas.

The conductor Walter Domroush (1862-1950), famous for his arrangement of the *Star-Spangled Banner* with John Philip Sousa, once stopped his orchestra in the middle of practice and asked, "Where is the seventh flute?" Not the second or the fourth but the seventh. The seventh flute played an important part in creating the harmony the leader desired. The moral: Each of us has a part to play and we need to do it well! No matter how incompetent or uncomfortable you feel about various parts of your job, such as administrative work, don't underestimate the importance of working to become more competent in your weaker areas if you plan to succeed. However, don't give up. Skills can be improved, but you must work at it. Now let's talk about how.

Tips to Improve and Become a Competent

First, let's talk about writing, a skill most people lack. Here is a writing tip from my colleague Lee Pound. Lee is a well renowned author, editor, and writing coach. You can reach him at lee@ leepound.com. Check it out.

Lee suggests when you are preparing an article, you eliminate weakening words like words ending in: ly, ing, or by, there is, there are, something, possibly, maybe, very, really or so.

After you write, go back and eliminate as many of the offending words and word endings as possible, then find another way to express yourself. Give it a try and you will be surprised!

For those who are not good at written or oral presentations, take writing classes (many available on line) to improve these learned skills or join Toastmasters (www.toastmasters.com) to improve your speaking and leadership skills. Don't forget to read your own writing or practice your speaking by using a tape recorder or the voice recorder on your smartphone. Listen or read your material and you will see for yourself. You will be amazed with the results after a little practice.

After all, practice makes perfect or at least accomplished. Perfect is not necessary, accomplished is the goal.

I like to use the analogy of algebra. At first, as a high school freshman, I had difficulty understanding the concept, but by sticking with it and asking for help along the way I soon got it and became an ace. The moral: Be patient and stick with the difficult parts and the results will come.

You will be amazed at how fast you improve and become more comfortable with both writing and speaking.

I have seen this time and time again. I may even be one of those. I listen and learn all the time.

Another example of an essential is the staff accountant or accounting exec who is consistently late in reconciling the monthly bank account, closing the books, or giving inaccurate reports. They might have issues with time management or setting priorities. Often, they get fired, no matter how good they are otherwise. Better to prioritize activities or find a job selling real estate on commission!

Here's another: Sales executives who don't turn in their reports on time, no matter how good they are. Management always has them on a blacklist, which means they will have a short career if they don't take steps to improve their admin skills.

A different approach: Let's compare a mediocre police patrolman great at filling out paperwork on time and communicating with the sergeant or lieutenant with a great cop who needs help with their reports or developing communication skills with management. Which one gets the edge? Who would you promote?

In most professions, the person who is good at admin work and at least adequate at their primary duties, such as sales or police work, has the edge. Check it out.

The ones who can do both are priceless.

What if you are one of these or managing the same?

If you ignore the problem, it will never go away.

Prima Donnas

Prima donnas are the divas or divos of the world. Excuse me, I don't want to be gender ignorant, but I don't know the proper designation for the male version of diva, so let's go with divo.

Again, people with exceptional talent are special and often need special attention. This does not mean they are special in all areas.

The specialty may be only one specific arena.

Prima donnas are not accustomed to cleaning up their own messes. Plenty of others will do that for them. On the other hand, we normally take care of our own missteps. We will talk about that next.

If you need a specific talent or work with a person who has that talent, you must learn how to work best with that person. Otherwise you risk upsetting the team continuity, underusing the talent already aboard, getting less than exceptional results and even getting fired. That's why they call you a manager.

How do we work with the prima donnas of the workplace to create the best results for all? Here are a few examples. Remember, when dealing with prima donnas, as with greyhounds or divas, experts and trainers tell you these high-strung animals need to be treated with special care to get the most out of them. That special treatment comes with caveats.

The solution is to treat them special, up to a point!

To do that, we must teach them to clean up their own messes without inconveniencing others in the meantime. That is rule number one. You do this in several ways.

First, what do they excel at? Next, where do they fall short or need help to achieve this excellence?

When you and they figure this out, insist that this level of excellence be maintained if special assistance is to be part of their program. Otherwise, they will not be on your team. Communication and expectations are essential for a great employment relationship.

If you are the prima donna or diva, you must also buy in that your special needs come at a price, a high level of performance in your area of excellence without exception or whining excuses. If you don't do this, you are just an incompetent with special talent. Too bad!

Next, what is the impact on other employees, as special treatment may cause morale issues. To avoid such issues, the other employees must understand that any so called special treatment is part of the employment agreement and the expectations that go with the agreement.

What happens when we have more than one prima donna?

Other problems may occur, especially with clashing personalities. High-strung personalities don't always get along with others of similar traits. This is where the "how comes" are in play. Here is how one person handles the prima donnas she works with.

As my example relates:

In my company the news talent and Sales Account Executives are the prima donnas. Five account executives garner over 10 million dollars for our station each year.

To carry such weight, you must be a go-getter, a type A personality, overbearing at times, who deserves to get their way. Each one is valuable to the company and they know it.

As sales and promotions coordinator, I deal with them when I need information or when they need me. By the way, I'm also responsible for $1 million dollars of non-traditional revenues. These are creative measures to help retain clients and give them the results they expect. Believe me, it keeps me busy. When I need results, I have to be the NAG.

How I handle it when I need information is to ask once with an e-mail and set up a reminder to pop up on their computer. The deadline is usually a 48-hour period. If this doesn't get a response, it's time to get personal and go to their desk. This is well past the deadline. Then I must remind them an hour later if I don't get a response.

Most of the time this works as they do understand responsibility!

When they need information from me, they use my approach so we all have a good understanding. What works for me works for them.

Often, I get this plea, "I need this in one hour or can you work on this while I'm out to lunch? (Unlike them I don't need a lunch break?) or can you get this to me quick?"

While I can beg, they really, really know how to beg!

The Value of Saying No

In the 6+ years I've worked here, I used to adhere to their timelines. Then I realized the exceptional effectiveness of using the all-powerful word NO. After that, we all learned to work effectively together.

In my experience, prima donnas will ask for the moon but not with malice. They have an air of confidence and believe they deserve that moon and unless you set the stage they expect you to drop everything.

Over the past year or so, I learned that when we say NO and set strict boundaries we make it work for all of us. They've learned to prepare their work requests earlier and I've learned to stop stressing myself out. The result is better work and production for all. That is the key.

NO is a difficult word to implement and should be used with caution and thought through with respect and confidence.

You may think of prima donnas as being arrogant. However, I see it in a different way. I think it's confidence (just pushed to the limit). My best piece of advice is work with an air of confidence and respect for what you do. Everyone will in turn respect you and your time.

The Value of Learning to be a Leader

Prima donnas and essential incompetents are not easy to deal with, but, as a leader, exhibiting leadership skills is essential to maintaining a harmonious workplace. Leadership is not a singular issue; it is about developing a team that will enable you to get favorable results. By the way, planning, monitoring and managing are a part of the process. Developing teamwork is the key.

Consistency and communication are the factors for both and if it doesn't work out someone must go. That can end up being you if your leadership skills are not satisfactory.

Better to refine your leadership skills. Being a leader is more than telling your staff what to do and expecting it to be done. I don't care what your management skills or style is as we are all different and lead in different ways.

Figure out which one you are most comfortable with and bone up on them. Read books; find others that possess the same outlook and go to work learning. Find out what it takes to be successful using your favorite and most comfortable approach.

Don't be afraid to adapt as your experience grows.

Don't worry, it's easy to find plenty of material. Check online, look for biographies, self-help books, and ask those you respect and admire for the way they handle such problems. Unless you want to invent a new management/leadership style (that will require much testing and failures) find one that fits your style and personality. It won't be hard.

Leadership and Mentor Training

One of the downfalls I see in companies and organizations is the lack of management or leadership training.

People are put in positions for a variety of reasons, told what to do and then either sink or swim. Often, they sink.

What Should We Do If We Are a New Manager?

A new manager can find a mentor with a style and record that they not only admire but who has a record of success.

Note: you can do this early (before you are appointed a manager) and have a head start. One caution, don't be enamored with the title of your mentor. That is not always a mark of success. People are put in positions and given titles just because. I can think of many reasons for people getting titles such as: get them out of the way, put them where they will do less harm, don't have anyone else, or are just coasting. Make sure they are into the game and have a solid record of success as a manager.

Toastmasters International is a great leadership training organization and they even give awards for those that fulfill the requirements.

PS: Toastmasters is not only a good place for new "wannabes" but also works for experienced managers who want to revitalize their careers.

I have yet to hear of a company or organization that does not encourage their staff to be a part of Toastmasters once they see the benefits. Many companies even have their own internal Toastmasters clubs.

What is a Mentor?

How about a story of a person who swam rather than sink? You know the sink or swim analogy! We'll call her "the girl with green eyes and a heart of gold."

This dates back a while to the start of her career. She had experience as a secretary, then administrative assistant before getting married and becoming the mother of a young daughter.

As a casual Jew, she always wanted to be more closely associated with her faith. The opportunity came when she joined a Temple mom and me program when her daughter turned nine months old. She enjoyed this and made a lot of friends and even volunteered to be the art teacher for the school.

Along the way, the school's director saw she handled not only the children but also the parents well. Soon the director had her teaching art and taking early childhood college courses and giving tours of the school to prospective parents. She enjoyed both the duties and the classroom learning in college.

You see, she was both personable and smart! Soon she became pregnant with her second daughter. She still talks about all the menial tasks she had to do, like being eight months along and having to sweep the school floors, then having to go back when told she missed a spot! We do what we need do. She managed and kept going to school, getting her credits and her admin degree.

She loved her job and performed well so after a few years the Temple asked her to open and run a new infant/toddler program for their school.

This is her first experience managing people and being responsible for the financials, including controlling costs and budgeting. At first these areas were a mystery to her and she was lost. But, as I said, she was smart and soon learned to get mentors. First her husband then the Temple treasurer were her mentors. She caught on quick but not without drama. It was always scary to predict revenues and costs when the Board of Directors was looking over your shoulder.

She was very successful and after a few years got the opportunity to run the pre-school at a nearby Temple. She handled this well and stayed for seven years. Along the way, she developed mentors in the financial area and learned and learned. The board, peers, parents, children, and employees loved her. Did I say she was smart? And she made the school profitable.

It was a big decision to leave the school she had grown and fostered for the past seven years, but an opportunity arose that she could not pass up. She was recruited by another growing Temple in a different part of the county. Reputations do get around.

It was scary, but I guess the seven-year itch is real and she had to scratch that itch.

The new Temple was in the process of erecting a new building and now she had to design and integrate a new school, a daunting task, and hire a new staff, get a student body, get licensed and convince the Board and parents that this was the correct move. She also had to convince the senior staff rabbis that she was more than a casual Jew.

Each one was an awesome undertaking.

Now this chapter is about mentoring and being a mentor so, let's get on to the rest of the story.

For the next 15 years, her job was to create the finest early childhood program possible. In that time, the school grew from 40 families that first year to an average of over 120 families in succeeding years. This meant full capacity with a waiting list. Results far exceeded initial expectations.

The school's reputation grew. Many of the families were not Jewish but had a desire for a great education for their children. The school became one of the largest in the Jewish community as well as respected throughout the secular community.

Early on she teamed with another director to start an all-inclusive program that focused on bringing special needs children into an atmosphere where they could grow and learn with kids not considered as having special needs issues. No other public or private school had this. You see, special needs kids are like the rest of us so called normal folks. While they had issues, they had the same needs and desires as everyone else. Even the public schools didn't offer a program like this. Their programs segregated the special needs kids from the regular student body.

While she didn't know much about outside financing, when they began the school project they received a grant from tobacco money along with other grant-giving organizations. The money allowed them to get a mentor and even parental assistance for those that needed financial help for aides.

Through the assistance of mentors, her knowledge, while not from formal education, became equal or better than trained experts. The public-school systems in their area always complimented what they did and often recommended parents to her program.

The difference was hands on experience rather than theoretical insight, again the value of having mentors. The difference is your mentor is like having your own private college professor who has practical experience in their area of expertise. Most college professors only have book knowledge, not actual experience.

Their program received national recognition and they were asked many times to speak to the National Association of Early Childhood Educators as well as to Early Childhood Educators in other countries. The results had a positive impact on hundreds of otherwise segregated students and families.

The program became known in both the public as well as the Jewish community. The parents of the special needs students were the biggest supporters as their children and families were the beneficiaries.

We've talked about the value of getting mentors to advise and help us succeed. How about becoming a mentor?

This requires more than just knowledge but also trust, being honest and forthright. The person you mentor must want it and be willing to listen then take the actions necessary to be successful.

Likewise, the mentor must realize their mentee is a separate person who needs to think out the issue and come up with a solution and action plan on their own. This is the hardest part of the job. Don't look over their shoulder. That is not mentoring; it is micro managing.

Make sure they know your thought process, but let them think it out for themselves. After all, if you were not around they would have to come up with a solution. Your mentoring should help that process. Make sure they understand they will find more than one right answer.

The question is choosing the best. This requires a sound thought process. Asking questions can refine this process.

How mentoring helped this lady with her early childhood career was the theme of this chapter and to go one step further, along the way she assumed the role of mentor. Early on it was in developing an association with other directors in the area. She was a founding member of this group. They would meet regularly at each of their sites to discuss issues facing each of the directors and how to handle matters like enrollment, parental issues, encouraging good practices in the various schools, training, funding, and a whole variety of matters. They developed an attitude of mentoring each other and this benefited not only the quality of education but the whole community.

You can also solicit opinions from others that have an interest in your success. You will then get a better idea how others see you. They may even give you suggestions that can be beneficial, even though you may not agree at first. Listen and don't be defensive. Just take what you can from it.

It is interesting that as I'm writing this book she is also writing a book on her experiences and lessons. The book is to be entitled *It was Never Just a Job* and focuses on encouraging young people about the values and rewards of the early childhood education profession. It will be awhile before publication, so keep an eye out for it.

She, over the years, made it a point to develop and mentor her own staff with the result that a number went on to make this a permanent career and others went on to become successful directors in other schools. This is called respect and encouragement to be the best you can be. It is a common trait among forward thinking managers. Hope you got good ideas out of the story of the girl with green eyes and a heart of gold.

By the way the Temple Treasurer not too long ago told her, "The temple will never realize how much you have meant to this Temple."

As a final point on mentoring, you can also solicit feedback from others that have an interest in your success. You will see how others see you. They may even give you beneficial suggestions, even though you may not initially agree. Listen and don't be defensive, just take what you can from it.

You can also be a mentor. The key is don't stick your nose in unless solicited and don't only give criticism. Praise goes a long way.

A good technique to use is the sandwich system: first comes praise, next give criticism or suggestions for improvement, and last, add more praise.

As for the sandwich? Praise is the bread that holds the sandwich together, criticism along with suggestions for improvement are the meat and cheese. End on an upbeat (complimentary) note.

The power of a compliment can change a person's life.

As far as compliments go, I'm told about a widow with five kids who was still young but had no intention of ever getting married again. After all, who would ever want a woman with five young kids?

While chaperoning a dance with one of her girls, she received an anonymous note complimenting her on how she was dressed and how good she looked. She went home and put the note on her refrigerator although she never knew who sent the note. This complimentary note changed her life and she became aware of how she looked, her presence, and outlook on life. She even started going to social events, maybe even in hopes of finding a new husband. Don't think she ever did, but it changed her life and elevated her self-esteem.

Never underestimate the value of a compliment or a use of positive words.

She never did find a new husband but kept that complimentary note on her refrigerator all those years. When she passed away, her daughter found a note to her among her mom's clothes. It said, "I knew you wrote that note."

Leaders/mentors have always found compliments work well. Just learn how to use them in the right manner. Do not be a panderer. Give this a try and see how this works for you.

Leadership: Teams and Teammates

What is the difference? Are they the same? I don't think so. Here is what I mean. Teams are made up of a group of people with different skills and attributes. Members may be called a team, but that does not make them teammates.

Teammates on the other hand are a group of people that work together to get results that benefit all, egos aside. These are two different things in my estimation. We see it every day on sports teams. A few win championships, most don't. Most often it is the teams that operate as teammates that win.

In 2014, the San Francisco Giants barely got into the baseball playoffs. They didn't win their Division championship, but the players operated as teammates and won the World Series! They did the same in 2012.

Do you think this was a coincidence?

You see, this is where leaders come into play. Leaders make the hard decisions that inspire others to make teams into teammates.

Did the Giants have the players with the most talent? No, plenty of other teams had higher payrolls, more talented players and better season records. Yet the Giants succeeded where the others didn't. The leadership inspired the players to come together as teammates and took the big one.

What I'm getting at is it takes leadership, teamwork and being teammates to succeed at the highest levels. Just like the restaurant chef, waiters, bus staff, dishwashers, etc. that I mentioned earlier. One person cannot do it alone. It takes teammates doing their job in an exemplary manner to be excellent.

Bill Belichek of the New England Patriots constantly urges his players, "Do your job well." Good advice for all of us.

OK, let's talk about that for a while and how leaders and teammates can make the difference.

Leaders do not ignore the little things as they get big results. It may by acknowledging your mates when you arrive in the morning, not just when you need help.

Teamwork will get stronger when you fulfill your role.

Don't wait until you have a complaint to speak up. It's not all about what's bugging you, it's about developing your teammates.

I was reading a story about the famous Movie Director Cecil B. DeMille. He was asked by a reporter after he had completed shooting the movie *The Ten Commandments*, "When did you get started on this Epic story?" He thought for a moment and replied, "The first day of my life!"

The moral: The things you do every day influence what you do today. Don't underestimate the value of your everyday activities. How you act every day is how you will influence your teammates and the people around you.

One more little tip, writing a short note in a timely manner can be very effective. It should be done in a timely manner and not well after the fact when the issue has been forgotten. And it should be without malice.

For a leader, developing teammates out of teams is an onerous task. I hope these concepts hit home for maybe you will be lucky enough to also win the World Series.

The Fallacy of Being Perfect

Have you ever wondered why other people seem to be better at a task than we are? Are they smarter, with better athletic endowment, better prepared, better motivated or just luckier? Do we hold off doing a task because of the fear of looking less than perfect or the thought that I'm just not good enough or I need to be perfect? Just how perfect do we have to be?

Here is an example of what being perfect before doing can lead to:

At 2012 presidential inauguration, singer Beyoncé thought she had to be perfect in singing the national anthem, so she decided to lip sync her rendition.

While most of the media ignored it and many said, "Who cares," others were appalled that she would fake it! Does this instance of fakery put a pox on her? Did she have to be perfect?

No. Perfection does not always lead to making the best performance or the best impression or even the best decision. You be the judge.

Innumerable superstar athletes have not come close to achieving even their best times (perfection) in the

Olympics, World Series, or other major sporting events. Yet many average athletes have excelled (perfection) way beyond their normal abilities during these events by using their talents and doing it. No need to worry about being perfect, just being good, really good will work out fine.

How do we judge ourselves? Do I have to be perfect before attempting to do a task? I hope not.

People think of a perfect marriage as being the ideal. How many do you think are perfect? Well, while many good ones exist, I can only think of one, Adam and Eve! Really, how so you ask? It's simple. Adam didn't have to hear about all the guys she could have married and Eve didn't have to hear about his mother's cooking! Object: We don't have to be too perfect to be good. However, while we don't have to be perfect to excel, we have to be pretty good!

In my last book, *Rekindling the American Dream*, I wrote about how to excel, and studies have shown that to be good at a task, really gooood, you must put in about 10,000 hours of exhausting time and effort to make it.

When it comes to being perfect, often that requires too much time and too many resources to achieve. By the time we get around to being perfect, our original goal may be not relevant. Dr. Ben Carson, the famous brain surgeon, talks about the constant studying during his career, point being we can and should always work to improve as very seldom are we perfect during our lives, at least not for long.

As they say, "Baby, it's too late." Just put in the time and effort to do your best and give it a try. Most of the time you don't have to be perfect to be good and the more you work on it and do it the better you will get.

You can find many examples, but, as I mentioned earlier, if you are a heart surgeon planning to do major surgery on me, I hope you are perfect. The rest of us for the most part don't need to be all that perfect.

The moral being: Trying to be perfect often leads to nothing ever getting done.

The next question is how good do we have to be and how do we make that happen?

Here are a few thoughts:

Never be content. Always strive to improve. This applies to all stages of life. However, don't let this stop you from doing. We learn from what we do. In fact, we learn more from doing than from contemplating or even practicing.

If our problem is one of contentment, the trouble is we always want more of it! This can keep us from being as good as we can be or need to be. It would be sad to say on our deathbed, if only I had done this or that but didn't because of the notion in our heads that we had done enough (contentment) or we needed to be perfect.

Frustration can be a big obstacle in our life and careers. Don't let that stop you from moving forward. Just because you did not do as well as you had hoped is not a reason to quit or stop trying to improve. Just let it go...as my old high school baseball coach used to say as I was complaining about being tired.

Think of Liz Taylor for a moment, with her 8 or 9 marriages. While she didn't seem to ever get it right, failure never deterred her; she at least kept trying for perfection. I think...

Here is a good technique to use: When an action you take does not achieve your desired results, do a recap.

Think of three items: 1) what went well, 2) what didn't go so well, and 3) what changes can I make. A suggestion, work on this recap as soon as you complete your project. It will be fresh in your mind and you will recall other important factors later. When we have desires and expectations and we want more and have less, frustrations can be debilitating, if we let them. Do yourself a favor and don't let them.

Near misses can be frustrating and lead to long term nightmares. Legendary golfers Sam Snead and Arnold Palmer always talked about the nightmares they had in not winning the fourth leg of golf's grand slam (Sam, the US Open and Arnie the PGA), this despite the fact they had near misses in each and each won more tournaments than any of their peers. Another example is Jim Kelly and the Buffalo Bills losing four consecutive Super Bowls. Note Jim is in the Football Hall of Fame even though he never won a Super Bowl and had a couple of near misses. He was however, a good quarterback.

When we have high expectations, results can be very elusive and as I heard can cause a tyranny of perfection to invade our mind. On the other hand, while we may not always achieve our goal, we are a whole lot better if we make the effort.

It can even be those that achieve less seem happier than those that just missed because of their need for perfection. For you, consider how far you need to go with how far you have come and how far you want to go.

Curiosity: If only we were as curious in our later years as when we were kids. Little kids seem to have the affliction of not being able to keep their hands off anything or giving us the endless task of answering their inane questions. Maybe it's all that rote learning in school that helps to remove the important curiosity trait from our beings. Could it be all the, "No, you can't do that!" Or the, "Don't touch that." Or, "Stay away from there." Or, "It's done this way," that helps us to stop being curious as kids. In my mind, we stop learning when we stop being curious.

Often it is the only one right way syndrome that helps stun our creativity and curiosity. A good exercise is to find more than one right way.

Has this ever happened to you?

In my gardening workshops, I often ask the audience why they do it this way or that way. Frequently the answer is, "Because that's the way my father did it or this is how I've always done it or this is how they taught me." Again, there goes the curiosity trait.

As we get older we have the tendency to stop experimenting and go with the familiar route rather than testing the boundaries. Have you ever noticed that?

Caution, before you attempt to make a major change, figure out how the existing system works. the ins and outs, the good and bad. When that is done, you will have a good understanding of how and why changes should be made.

Just because the existing system seems clumsy or old fashioned is not good enough.

Making changes is not easy until you find a better way.

A suggestion is to strive to learn new skills and take on new ideas and methods. By challenging yourself and daring to learn new information or techniques, you will retain your sense of curiosity all your days.

Hint, you can start by opening your mind to a skill you always wanted to do but never had the means or the ability to try. Just ask yourself, what is the worst that can happen and see for yourself.

Give you an example of myself. The Orange County Master Gardener program had an opportunity to create a public interest radio program with University of California Irvine's public radio station. They asked for volunteers to host the program.

While I have never done anything like that, I volunteered. The consideration being the requirement of attending an eight-week extended class training program through the university then passing a university test as well as a FCC test. It would have been much easier to let another person do it.

Was it a challenge? You bet. I passed the rigid tests and our program called *In the Garden* is in its third season and has been expanded to a one-hour weekly format with a growing audience. We have almost 100 programs in the vault on the way to the public radio Hall of Fame.

Now my friends say Mark, you have the perfect face... for radio.

My advice is to ignore the adage that practice makes perfect. Practice does not always make perfect, especially if what you are practicing is the wrong way. However, doing the task the right way and practicing helps.

You will find the more you do it, the better you will get. So, don't be content, put your frustrations aside and let your curiosity take over.

When Our Dreams Go South

Good times come often in our lives. They may last for a long while, then one thing or another occurs and our dreams seem to all be bad and we go into what appears to be a dry spell or funk.

Often when we try to follow our dreams, they don't go as we planned or hoped and we end up in a less than ideal situation. What we do after that makes a difference. Perhaps it's a result of having the wrong dream or the wrong idea or the idea is not fully vetted. The question is, "How do we get back on track?

Maybe it's the dry spell that starts after graduation and we must adapt to a new time in our life. We didn't realize school was such a good time until it was over.

Maybe it started when we get our first job out of school, got a promotion, or when we are recognized for an action we took, got an award, got married, had children, and on and on.

(Note: I recently went to a college reunion. One of the honorees made a comment. He stated that he was reluctant to receive awards and gave four reasons for his reluctance: They normally are given to a person who is retiring, about to retire, is dying, or about to die.)

Think back and you will recall the good times in your life. It's better when we receive recognition for what we've done. This is important as sooner or later difficult times will wind their way into your being. That's part of life. As the saying goes, "Into each life some rain must fall."

What Can We Do?

Here are a few thoughts on dealing with the good times as well as the times that are not so good or when our dreams seem to go bad:

Don't take them for granted or think you deserve or are entitled to good times all the time. While we don't ever want to anticipate bad events, it helps to be prepared. That's why we have insurance, to help us overcome disasters big and small, and we all know how wealthy the insurance companies are.

Yes, almost everyone has insurance, for health, our cars, our homes and household possessions, and whatnot. Even the insurance companies have insurance. They're called reinsurers. Yes, insurance companies have insurance to help modify the risk.

You can do the same to modify the risk by starting now to make plans (insurance) in event that a disaster arises in your life.

I remember many years ago, when a young (at the time) insurance agent friend of mine, Doug McCowen, reminded me that it's not if, but when! Thanks, Doug. Being prepared is not looking on the down side but looking ahead.

It's as simple as developing a savings plan that will insure you are on sound financial ground in event of a setback.

A good qualified, licensed financial adviser can help lead you in the right direction. How about continuing your education, developing a good networking group or groups?

Spend time cultivating your soul, your body, friends, and finances. These will be your personal insurance policies.

Here is a short story to emphasize the point for dealing with hard times. One day, Mark Twain was coming out of a church with a friend. It was raining cats and dogs and his friend asked, "Do you think it will ever stop?" Mark Twain replied, "It always has!"

Attitude Counts

Often, it's difficult to keep a positive outlook when everything seems to be upside down. Here are a few keys to help us keep a positive outlook during difficult periods:

Start by making a list of the blessings in your life. Keep it updated as it's an uplifting experience.

Suggestion: When you are first making this list, make sure you have quiet time. The object is not to be distracted.

Start making your count your blessings list by beginning with now and go back in time. Go back as far as you want and don't be too selective. Write down the blessings in your life today, and proceed backward in time. A wise man once said, "You never know you have blessings until you count them." You will be surprised how much good is a part of your life. A person once told me, maybe my Mom, you don't learn from winning, only from losing.

We learn from our mistakes and can then take steps to improve on our deficiencies. It's amazing what we can learn by taking classes, finding a mentor, or asking questions of a person you respect and listening to what they say. This approach will help in maintaining a good positive, balanced approach to life. Discouragement is a tool of the devil. Endure your trials and don't yield to the devil. Count your blessings instead of sheep!

Other Benefits

Keeping and maintaining a positive mental approach can do much not only for us but for the people who surround us. It helps the way others look at us and the way we look at ourselves.

Who you rather associate with, a person who has a rosy outlook or one who is all about woe is me? Sympathy is not what we are about, encouragement is and that begins with us and the people with whom we associate.

It's like this: One day while on the golf practice range I asked a great golfer friend of mine about his practice routines and why he practices so much. His reply was simple, "It seems the more I practice, the luckier I get!"

The late, great motivational speaker and sales trainer Zig Ziglar liked to say, "Your attitude, not your aptitude, will determine your altitude." Another one from Zig, "There is very little traffic on the extra mile."

I like that one. My interpretation is: "Good judgment comes from experience and experience comes from bad judgment." I don't know who said this, but it is true. We learn from our mistakes and experience.

Maybe it's a good time to talk about planning. How do we begin this task? While many books cover the subject as well as many theories, here are a few ideas that may help. Begin by deciding what you want to accomplish and the strategies and tactics you will need to achieve your goals. This will tell you whether your plan is realistic or a pipe dream.

Strategies are what you want to do and tactics are what you need to do to get there. "It's like the old joke, "How do you eat an elephant?" Strategy is that I want to eat an elephant. Tactic is one bite at a time! Note, strategy without tactics is meaningless. Tactics without a strategy is a waste of time and energy.

First you must have goals. Setting realistic, achievable goals along with a timetable is the hardest task. My friend, fellow writer, and career coach John Hall, (an all-around superstar in the career development field) will insist on specifics and makes his clients be specific down to what time of day they will have it done. And he holds them to it.

He says, "It's one thing to say it, another to do it." Remember what I said earlier. To win the lottery, you first must buy a ticket. Strategy is to win the lotto, tactics are how many tickets you need to buy and what numbers to pick. Hope this is not too simple, but I think you get the point. By the way, I haven't won the big one yet, guess I'm not playing often enough or picking the right numbers!

Ken Blanchard, Author of *One Minute Manager* and Tom Peters, author of *In Search of Excellence,* talk about setting goals as a manager and following up along the way.

To ensure you are on the way to being successful with your goal setting, make it a point to set a regular time for measuring how you are doing. Adjust along the way. After all, when plans get in the way of living, methods and objectives must be amended from time to time.

Frequently, we focus on one area and ignore a key section that is critical in planning for times that may be more challenging. It's like time for spring cleaning, time to change the batteries in our smoke detectors, or time to change the oil in our vehicle.

Making the time to clean out the attic or the garage should be one of those plans. It gets rid of the clutter.

Speaking about cleaning out the attic, maybe we should focus on that for a while. When we go up there, we find all kinds of items that have either been forgotten, intended to keep for later use, or just no longer find relevant.

If you are like me, most go in the trash, are saved for sentimental value, or given away to those that need them.

Work at it all the time. Work hard on your attitude, go the extra mile, and the luckier you will get.

Here's another way to look at it. This is kind of inane as it does not involve working hard, but it does involve acting.

If I were to win the lottery, would it be just a stroke of good luck or a result of an action I took? How did I do it? Just by random luck or did I first select the numbers and then go buy a ticket. The price of inaction is you will never win the lottery if you do not act and buy a ticket, even if it's a remote chance.

Have you heard about the man who went to church every Sunday and while there prayed to God, "Lord, I have been good all week. Can you do me a favor and let me win the lottery?" Each week he would repeat the same request, telling the Lord he had been good all week and asking him to let him win the lottery. Then one day, after months of making his weekly visit and request and still not getting results, one Sunday after church he sat alone and made another plea. From the eaves of the church rafters, he heard a refrain, "I'm trying, but you got to buy a ticket!"

Your blessings are a result of an action you took. Not all our actions get the results we want, but planning and action do play a part.

Remind yourself how blessed you are. Remember that old song that goes like this, "When I'm worried and I can't sleep, I count my blessings instead of sheep." A thought to ponder. I hope you keep that positive outlook and may you sleep restfully.

Keeping at It

I don't know about you, but I'm not very easy to be around when I am not working on a project with a good plan as to how I will get it done (although my wife would say I'm not easy even when I do, she still puts up with me).

I've found it's a good idea to set goals for myself then make a backup plan. A good friend and fellow member of our writer's group, Steve Amos (engineer by profession), emphasizes the necessity of when suggesting change to come up with more than one plan. I don't know if this is scientific in theory, but often we will find more than one right way to solve the problem. By exploring various solutions, you can come up with the best solution.

This ensures that you have thought through the problem and have come up with more than one right alternative. The old Jewish saying goes like this, "Man plans and God laughs." The best laid plans *Of Mice and Men* yield to what happens in the real world. Even the best generals always have backup plans. They all know in the heat of battle even the best of plans go up in smoke when the fighting begins. Good preparation is to have more than one plan.

The same applies to our mind. The time comes when we need to clean out our mind's attic. We can get away without doing any of these for a while, but soon these lapses catch up with us. Updating our plans and adding new ones when changes occur, even deleting those that are no longer relevant, will help with our peace of mind and well-being.

Where should we be perfect or what should we strive for? My answer is: It depends! Note: this is an answer I often provide when giving gardening workshops and an audience member asks me a question like, "How come I can't seem to grow a good crop of tomatoes?"

To give a proper answer, I need to know more, like soil conditions, time you are planting, what has grown there before, sun conditions, light, watering practices, species, seed conditions and numerous other variants.

An answer to an open-ended question like this often requires more information. For example, if you are a rocket scientist sending people to the moon, you need to be close to perfect. If you are a heart surgeon where being perfect means whether your patient lives or dies, you have no room for being less than perfect. You had better be well trained, have good credentials and technique, and be on your game that day (at least if you were planning on working on me!)

As a final thought, while we don't always have to be perfect, we must be good at what we do. We can be by taking the time to plan and putting in the effort to make it be as perfect as we want it to be. Normally we are too lazy to go beyond the one perfect answer. That is human nature.

Reread my chapter on *The Fallacy of Being Perfect.*

Code of Conduct

Almost everything we do has consequences. Our actions may be right or wrong, good or bad. The problem is each action or decision often brings up an unclear ethical dilemma.

If we consider ourselves to be ethical, but the right or wrong, good or bad of an action is unclear, how do we steer our thoughts and decisions in the direction that will avoid harmful consequences? Since I first took ethics in one of my required college classes, the question, "Am I doing the right thing?" has always been a part of my decision-making process.

PS: Like in my last chapter, I have not always done or made the right or perfect decisions. Maybe I'm too lazy.

As I said, one does not have to be perfect. Here are a few of the concepts I have used over the years to help in making decisions in the code of conduct process.

We all are familiar with the golden rule. It means avoiding consequences that hurt others without sacrificing our own interests. It should be reasonable and contribute to the general good. If you follow that theme, you will be on the right track.

Think along the lines of being a member of the community and not as an individual. This theme involves the rules of fairness and propriety that allow you and others to prosper. Respecting contracts, just debts, and selling decent products at reasonable prices should be a part of not only our makeup but the business community as well.

Being an ethical person goes beyond following the law or legal compliance. After all, many things are not illegal but are unethical. One that comes to mind is taking advantage of trust. I'm sure you can think of other actions that are not illegal but are unethical.

Obeying moral rules is a basis of making ethical decisions both on a personal as well as business basis. No exceptions, even if you think you can get away with it. Moral rules count. Do good even if nobody else knows about it.

Be objective in your thinking. Look at it from a neutral viewpoint. This will help you to determine if it is truly right or just a rationalization of self-interest that gives a good excuse for many in justifying their actions.

Be sure to separate feelings and logic. At times, we feel one way, but if we think about it logically we can see that is the wrong way to think.

A good question to ask if in doubt is, "What type of person would do such a thing?" As someone once said to me, ethics is not about obedience to rules but about the up-keep of your personal character. This goes for your personal as well as business dealings. After all, your good name is important. Often, it's hard to do the right thing when you don't know what the right thing to do is. However, you will when the time is right.

The late Peter Drucker of the Drucker Institute at Claremont University summarized it as, "Being able to look at your face in the mirror in the morning." Not bad!

Over the past 20 or so years, we have become a global society. From an ethical standpoint, respect for other people that don't look like us, speak like us, or have the same customs as we do is essential to our overall wellbeing. Studying other cultures will be a great benefit in your career. As the old saying goes, "when in Rome" is a good rule of thumb unless it violates your moral values. Always stick with your principles.

Grappling over doing the right thing and being able to look yourself in the mirror will never be cut and dried.

Guess we live with it and do our best to make our mothers proud.

Stress: Let's spend a moment on this bad boy as stress is one of the biggest mysteries in life. In my mind, stress can be either a killer or a motivator.

We prefer it to be the latter rather than the former. With good times being the theme, let's focus on how we can use it in a positive manner.

Let's start out by playing it smart. Smart, in this case, does not mean being brain smart. It is more like being street smart. Street smart is having the ability to keep your eyes and ears open to what is going on around you all the time.

I love to read police mystery novels. They intrigue me. The reason being the best police detectives can figure out the inanest situations to solve a crime. Does that make them smarter than the average bear? Probably not. In fact, they are often beset by other parts of their personality.

These may include too much alcohol, anger, impatience, or difficulties in relationships. What they do have is the ability to stay focused in the most complex of situations. Focus and observance of details lead them to the perp that committed the perfect crime.

By the way, Michael Connelly's Harry Bosch novels and the Alex Cross series are two of my favorites.

How will this help us deal with stress? While I'm not a trained psychologist, a few of my thoughts might move you.

Confidence in your ability is a great starting point. Your training and years of experience help create a measure of confidence even if you are (in your opinion) in over your head.

I can remember when as a young lad (15) on my town team's baseball squad I always felt overmatched.

Our team played in a high semi-pro level league that included many ex-professional players, including major leaguers along with many current college players.

Here I was, a 15-year-old high school pitcher with not much of a fastball. One Sunday afternoon as I rode my bike to the town's baseball diamond, I wondered what I was doing there. It wasn't so much nervousness as not being sure of my ability to compete against a group of opposing players who I thought were much better than me.

In other words, I was in over my head. I had to figure out how I was going to get through this. As I was riding, I said to myself, "Just get the first darn pitch over the plate and take it from there." We won that day and I made it a practice from then on to take it one pitch at a time no matter what I was doing. Likewise, I always found it best throw fast balls and no curves in your business career. That also goes well in life. Be honest. While I will say as I got older I had a decent fastball along with a devastating curve ball.

You learn to throw only fastballs and you will have a happier and more fulfilling life. When your colleagues learn you only throw fastballs and no curves, your esteem in their eyes skyrockets.

When you are in a situation where your confidence needs bolstering, break your large goal into a series of small ones and when you achieve each small goal you will gain a sense of accomplishment. The result is a series of small goal accomplishments that will grow your confidence and lead to completion of the larger goal. Almost like that age-old saying, "How do you eat an elephant?" One bite at a time. Try it out and see for yourself (I don't mean the elephant!). You may want to consider self-talk in the same tone we would use to talk to a small child. We are harder on ourselves than is appropriate so be kind to yourself.

After confidence, consider your outlook. Consider taking the upbeat approach. Instead of it being a problem, consider it as an opportunity. Consider the Chinese character for Crisis, which includes both the characters for danger and for opportunity. It's like the person who hated her new job because the people she worked with were horrible to her. None of them were friendly to her nor would help her. She considered quitting the job she hated so much. She explained her situation at work to an old friend outside of work. The friend suggested that every occasionally, maybe once per week, she bring in a box of doughnuts for the people in her work crew. Several weeks later the friend asked her how it was going at work and she said, "Everything is great. They have changed so much!" Oh, yeah.

Normally, I would not include this section, but since I wanted to get across several important points, I have included it.

Summary of Chapter:

It's what we do after a bad situation that makes a difference.

Always think back and focus on the good times in your life.

Don't take the good times for granted. We are not entitled to good times all our lives.

Being prepared is not looking on the downside, it's looking ahead.

Keep a positive outlook during difficult times.

Make a list of the blessings in your life and update them frequently. Think about them often.

Associate with people that have a rosy outlook.

Work at getting better all the time. The harder you practice, the luckier you will be.

Go the extra mile. Don't worry, the traffic is light on that extra mile.

Your attitude, not your aptitude, will determine your altitude.

Generally, your blessings are the result of something you did.

Keep a positive outlook and get restful sleep.

Set your goals and make a backup plan.

Having more than one plan ensures you have thought through the issue.

There is always more than one right answer.

Decide what you want, then the strategies and tactics needed to accomplish it.

Be specific.

Follow up.

Adjust along the way.

When spring comes, it's time to clean our mind's attic. Maybe summer, fall and winter, too.

Update our plans and delete the ones no longer relevant. Gives peace of mind.

Do I have to be perfect? I hope not. Not all the time anyway.

If we don't have to be perfect, we must be good to excel.

Put in the effort to be as perfect as we want.

Almost everything we do has consequences.

Follow the Golden Rule.

Be a good member of the community. Keep your personal character in order so you can look at your face in the mirror.

Always stick to your principles.

Smart doesn't always mean brain smart. Be more street smart.

Work on dealing with daily stress.

Have confidence in your innate ability.

Take it one pitch at a time.

Break your large goals into a series of smaller ones to gain a sense of accomplishment.

Consider taking the upbeat approach. Make it not a problem but an opportunity.

Reflect on the issues and see your nightmares turn into good dreams.

Linear Vs Three-Dimensional Thinking

Why should I care, what do I mean and what's the difference? Let's think about it for a minute.

Linear thinking is what we learn in school from our teachers and professors and in books. It is the basis of our knowledge and how we come to conclusions.

When it comes to making decisions, linear thinking skills can be very beneficial in coming up with answers.

In the classroom, it helps create a format to solve complex issues. Mathematical problems and are good examples of linear thinking.

That's why our professors want us to memorize algebraic formulas, or in medical school understand bone structure, symptoms of complex diseases, and how they work.

Engineers, doctors, and math experts are good linear thinkers. The great ones also can think in three dimensions.

What is three-dimensional thinking?

It is what I call a soft skill. For example, being able to think out problems that don't fit the norm is the value of three-dimensional thinking. This can be very helpful when you attempt to improve a process.

Studies have shown the amount of education a person has is no indicator of how successful a person will be at three-dimensional thinking.

That would indicate to me that three-dimensional thinking ability is more important than the linear process. I don't know that for sure as I didn't have access to the studies that came to that conclusion. However, I wouldn't be surprised that a good balance of both would yield interesting results. Here we go. Just as the scribblings in a book on war are not the same as making decisions in the heat of battle, it is good to know what it says in the book.

It helps to have a good basis as learned in the linear classroom. When life and changing circumstances come into play, three-dimensional thinking goes above and beyond the usual. As my colleague, John Hall, says, "Everything is not black and white and anyone that thinks so is mistaken."

Unfortunately, many professors acknowledge only one right way, their way. Even Einstein, if he were your teacher, would agree. The ability to think outside the box is the most valuable asset you can have, but you need to back it up!

As a side note, recently modern techniques, technology and scientists confirmed that Einstein's theory on gravity waves is true. This after 100 years! Yes, even science can have its differences.

I like to think of it as the difference between looking and seeing. It's like street smarts. Some people have them, some don't. They may look but don't see. On the other hand, you can refine that skill by focusing on what you are looking at. Then maybe you will see! I heard an analogy about smart. Seems many people think smart and clever are the same. However, they miss a significant difference. Smart is the ability to see the problem. Clever is the ability to solve it!

My suggestion is to take your professors or mentors seriously. While they don't have all the answers, listen to them, ask questions, and you may learn a thing or two.

I don't want you to think I'm downplaying the value of a good education. Absolutely not. In fact, learning is essential, learning to think is priceless!

Another quip from a colleague, engineer Steve Amos, that I have used before is, "When you are working on solving a problem, come up with more than one solution." That will ensure that you have thoroughly thought out the issue. Often, coming up with just one solution is lazy. Going further ensures you are exploring all the alternatives. A better solution could be just a matter of going a bit further, that is using both three dimensional and linear thinking.

To give you one more thought, companies and organizations big and small are constantly sending both their mid-level and senior managers to developmental seminars. The purpose is to not only enhance their ability to think outside the box but to develop a pattern of teamwork and problem solving skills that benefits all.

Have you ever been to one of these events where you break into small groups and are asked to come up with solutions or maybe team up on a physical experience that requires the trust of other teammates then give a recap to the rest of the seminar attendees to find out what each gained from the practice? It's an interesting experience.

These are linear thinking and three-dimensional sessions that require trust and input from others to be successful.

Some People Exist, Some People Live

Growing up, I thought that having fun was the most important thing to strive for. Have fun all your life was my goal as a kid! Fun is good, don't get me wrong, and I suppose that's the way kids think. Along the way, I found more to life than having fun.

How did this come about?

Simple, for most of my time I have been around people who influenced me to believe it is better to live than to just exist.

The older I got the more apparent it was that for me to more than just exist I was going to have to make a living, like getting a job.

Then would come the fun, or so I thought at the time. Here are my thoughts:

What I learned is that taking on responsibility or getting a job did not mean giving up fun or joy. More often it was a way to find it, almost like living instead of just existing. That brings up another point that I wish to emphasize, as we already have the ingredients to help us live.

It is well known that everybody needs someone in this world to believe in them. This can be friends, family or a higher being. Look upon it as a gift. As a unique individual, we all have many gifts:

Family is a gift. Even though we can't choose them, value them.

Friendship is a gift. Value your friends.

Strong faith and belief in God is a gift. Be thankful, it will give you strength in trying times. An old Jewish saying goes like this: God will never forget about you.

Giving to benefit others is a gift. Give and you will receive.

Cherish and foster these gifts and you will live rather than just exist. Giving to or helping others is and can often be greater fun and joy than receiving. Try it and see for yourself.

As John Hall said when I was telling my business and communications group colleagues about this chapter, a recent study he was reading showed that once you reach a certain level of income, you have no increase in happiness! Guess that means that having all the money in the world does not include the gift of family, friends or belief in a greater being.

I don't know where John got this study, but I guess I haven't reached that level of income yet. Maybe one day but, I do know the value of giving, family, friendship, and faith has made for a happy me.

One final little ditty. The other morning I was driving and casually listening to the 60s station on my radio. A song came on that I hadn't heard in years, and a few lines stuck with me.

"I feel it in my fingers,

I feel it in my toes

Love is all around us, everywhere we go"

That's it. I just figure that if we keep that thought in mind, maybe our world will be a better place!

This book and the others I have written are about my experiences that have affected me over the course of my life.

Hope my babblings will be useful. Thank you for making it all the way through. Mark Fierle, Author.

Get to Know Mark Fierle

After graduating from Gannon University in Erie, PA, he worked in management of finance areas for two Fortune 500 firms and later two large international companies.

Along the way, he was promoted to the West Coast where he was later recruited to join a large privately held service company as Assistant to the President. He later became President and soon after Chairman of the Board.

From there he entered the world of Executive Search and after a few years started his own firm. Soon he began writing articles on career-oriented subjects for a division of the Wall Street Journal along with speaking to networking groups and graduate level classes as a guest speaker.

One of his major side interests has always been gardening. A few years ago, he applied to and was accepted into the University of California Master Gardener Orange County program. He is now a Gold Badge member, part of the Speakers Bureau, founding President of the Orange County Toastmaster Gardeners Club and is a certified talk show host on the Master Gardener radio show *In the Garden*. The show is aired weekly on www.kuci.org in Irvine. He is a Certified Square Foot Garden Teacher. Vegetable gardening in small spaces is one of his specialties. His books include co-author of *Adapt or Perish* and author of *Rekindling the American Dream*. By the way if you are interested he has begun work on his next book, *What Comes Next?* Look for it in late 2017 if not sooner. His books can be purchased in e-book or softcover form on www.amazon.com. He can be reached at mfassoci@aol.com.